Social Work
and
Sexual Problems

A Practical Guide for Social Workers

by Judith Milner

Senior Lecturer in Social Work
Huddersfield Polytechnic

ISBN 0 948680 05 9

The Author

Judith Milner is a Senior Lecturer in Social Work at Huddersfield Polytechnic where her main teaching responsibilities are in human growth and behaviour and educational social work.

She came into social work originally in 1963 when she obtained a post as Mental Welfare Officer in Kingston-upon-Hull. She continued in mental health social work in London, Cardiff and Liverpool until going to Nigeria. She spent two years there and worked as a primary school teacher.

After the birth of her daughter, she returned to England where she obtained a divorce and a post as Senior Social Worker with Kirklees Social Services Department. After joining the Social Work Section at Huddersfield Polytechnic in 1977, she qualified as a teacher in further education.

She has been very happily remarried for 10 years to a wonderful man who shares her enthusiasm for Yorkshire cricket and her passion for trout and salmon fishing. She feels that her lifestyle qualifies her to comment on sexual behaviour but she acknowledges that many Freudians would interpret her hobbies as some sort of weakness in her oedipal development. This does not worry her at all, not least because it gives the students lots of material for the Christmas Review.

Dedication

To Mrs E. Lodge, who encouraged me to write this book.

Acknowledgements

I should like to thank all the social work students, past and present, at Huddersfield Polytechnic. Without their fascinating questions, their willingness to share their case material and their enthusiasm about tackling difficult cases, this book could never have been written.

Also, my family must take a large part of the credit. They have support- ed me throughout the writing of this book and have been constantly encouraging. A special thank you must go to my husband who has risked his reputation by collecting not only piles of books on sexual aberrations from the local hospital library, but also some very odd looks from the librarian.

Judith Milner
August, 1986

Contents Guide

Introduction

There are hundreds of books addressing all aspects of human sexuality and endless documentaries and discussion programmes on television; so why write yet another book on the subject? My reason is simply that there is no single authoritative and practically helpful book for social workers which offers advice on how to cope with the dilemmas involved in helping, changing and controlling aspects of human sexuality. I came to this conclusion rather slowly. In 1977, after sixteen years as a practising social worker, I moved into social work lecturing and found myself plunged into teaching about human sexuality on a social work course. My reluctance to face the fact that many of the experts actually know very little about the subject probably arose from reluctance to teach in this area. I certainly didn't volunteer but, like most new teachers, inherited it as part of many unpopular bits of the teaching programme. My colleagues rationalised their decision that I should teach the subject by pointing out that I had easy access to the relevant and specialist literature on the subject as my husband is a GP!

So I dutifully raided the psychiatric section of the local hospital library, borrowed everything that seemed vaguely relevant from the psycho-sexual counselling section of the Family Planning Association library, and persuaded my husband to hand over his copies of the British Journal of Sexual Medicine as soon as they arrived. Not too difficult, this one; he doesn't read it. Sensibly, he believes in starting at the "person end" of sexual problems presented in his surgery, not the "sexpert end". Determined to research and detail the "sexpert" view, I amassed an enormous amount of information and began lecturing on the subject. I might well have continued delivering standard lectures on the classification and aetiology of perversions, deviations and illnesses if it had not been for my students' questions. The very first question was from a probation student who described a case he had been allocated on placement - "What would I advise him to do with a man who had lost his testicles in an industrial accident and had since taken to stamping on women's feet whilst out shopping?

Could this be a fetish directly linked to the involuntary surgery or was it indicative of severe emotional disturbance due to the trauma of the accident?" Hmmm...well...

And this wasn't an atypical question. The students frequently found that they had to deal with complex, and often bizarre, sexual problems in placement. Like me, they were "landed" with work others avoided. Odd, isn't it, that my colleagues and agency professionals were so strongly avoiding of a subject which is generally considered not only to be no longer taboo but also one which we are often considered to be obsessed about? Are we as comfortable with our sexuality as we make out and do we understand the vast range of sexual behaviour that exists? I suspect not. "Surely, Judith," say my colleagues, "you don't really need to lecture on transvestism and transsexualism? They must be fairly rare and we could spend the time saved on more lectures on non-accidental injury?" Well, actually, they are not rare according to the students and whilst there is now acknowledgement of the high incidence of sexual abuse of children, our students have been handling incest cases regularly. And recent research into the handling of sexual problems in the Probation Service (Crolley and Paley, 1982) found the reluctance to take on such cases was such that, where transfer was impossible, the other strategies typically used were "helplessness, inactivity and other forms of doing nothing".

And the social work role in sexual problems is a particularly difficult one. As I write this, the Yorkshire Post (February 8th, 1986) - not one of the more lurid Sunday papers - reports on a man accused of unlawfully wounding, attempted kidnapping, and unlawfully administering chloroform and sleeping tablets with intent to assault his wife. He has received a five year gaol sentence. In mitigation, his defence counsel says it is a pathetic case. Here we have a man who entertained sexual fantasies about seeing his wife unconscious and whose car was found to contain a collection of tools, including a stanley knife, hammer, saw, syringe, bottle of chloroform and a length of rope, described as pathetic - what an understatement. Five years in prison - inadequate and unhelpful! Think for a moment about the tasks facing the probation officer assigned to undertake this man's prison aftercare and the social worker handling the wife's destruction of confidence in marital relationships. What book would you recommend for their guidance?

It is difficult to start even classifying this man in either accepted legal or psychiatric terms. Indeed, within one supposedly authoritative book on the pathology and treatment of sexual deviation, two completely incompatible classification models are described. Scott (1964), defining the field from a psychiatric point of view, suggests that sexually deviant behaviour falls into three main groups:

i) that not requiring a human partner, e.g. fetishism, bestiality, transvestism, transsexualism, asphyxia;

ii) that not requiring a willing partner, e.g. voyeurism, frotteurism, exhibitionism, paedophilia; and

iii) that requiring a willing partner, e.g. homosexuality, incest, paedophilia.

James (1964) outlines a legal classification - again in three groups, although this is the only similarity to Scott's classification:

i) offences against the accepted standards of family life, e.g. bigamy, incest, adultery, fornication;

ii) offences which display the normal sex drive in a distorted or unacceptable manner, e.g. rape, indecent assault on a woman, unlawful sexual intercourse, sexual murder, paedophilia, prostitution; and

iii) offences which display a perverted sexual drive, e.g. homosexuality, lesbianism, fetishism, voyeurism, exhibitionism, bestiality, sodomy with a woman, necrophilia, sadism, making obscene phone calls.

Patently absurd, are they not? Although, like me, you may delay in scornfully discarding them because they are presented by prestigeful experts and you are probably still puzzling over what frotteurism could possibly be or what on earth is the difference between adultery and fornication. Also, one tends to work from experts' classifications because it is so difficult to devise better ones, largely because consent is difficult to define within marriage and the family and because differing social definitions of "perversions" and "deviations" cloud the issue. For example, nudity is involved in stripping, streaking and exhibitionism, but these behaviours attract different degrees of social censure. And social censure levels don't remain constant - just as homosexuals obtain a degree of social acceptance, along comes AIDS and a moral backlash to put all but the brave back into the closet.

Also, it is almost impossible to establish what variant behaviour actually is when it is so difficult to establish even a baseline for "normal" heterosexual behaviour. When people respond to researchers' questions about frequency of sexual intercourse per week, do they mean every week (what about menstruation?), an average week, the number of sessions or the number of ejaculations/ orgasms? Ideal norms seem to exist but in no way do they reflect actual norms which encompass an infinite variety of human sexual responses. Gross deviations from the norm are easy to decide upon, but a completely "normal" sex life does not appear to exist.

Such a heavily researched subject really should be better under- stood, even though it is difficult to assess completely behaviour which is usually private, often secret, and sometimes only exists in fantasy. Also, our understanding is further clouded by the extremely male bias of most of the literature. The British Journal of Sexual Medicine is still trotting out the same boring articles it did eight years ago and still answering readers' questions about the importance of penis size (they mostly say it doesn't matter but they do express doubts . . .) and men becoming impotent when they suffer heart disease or get a female boss at work. I am rapidly coming to the conclusion that an understanding of human sexuality will not be furthered as long as the literature remains the province of men, written by them, about them and for them. Certainly, most sexual offenders are men but men cannot satisfactorily explain their own sex's behaviour. Gosselin and Nielson (1984), commenting on fetishism and sadomasochism, say:

> .... the surprising specificity and inflexibility of the
> basis for sexual arousal that is seen in many variant
> males . . . seems to implicate some form of imprinting.

They cannot accept conditioning, so it might be biological. Why should males be so much more susceptible to biological events than women, whose bodies are just as complex? Apart from a very few books (Davies 1984, Plummer 1981), male writers tend to ignore social and emotional issues involved in human sexuality and attempt to be scientific, rational and objective. This is quite impossible until they acknowledge that they are writing from a male perspective and that issues about male power in society may have some influence on behaviour. I thought, therefore, that a book by a woman (albeit a mild feminist) might be helpful. Mine is also unashamedly a social work perspective; I think this is useful as social workers have to accept that they are involved in changing and controlling behaviour as well as in helping people. As Hart (1981) argues, social workers cannot help but act as moral agents in determining good and bad conduct in a manner which reinforces their views. For example, a social worker's views about incest would determine whether an incestuous father was recom-mended for punishment or therapy, whether he was allowed back with the family or whether the victim was removed. Variant and dysfunctional sexual behaviour is only truly maladaptive in an evolutionary sense (Beach 1977) but it is harmful in its social and emotional context. The damage caused in this context is what concerns social workers and this is what I hope to concentrate on.

I said earlier that I do not consider that there is one authoritative book on the subject, although male readers, alarmed by the feminist perspective hinted at in this book, may wish to stop now and read Trimmer (1978) (the best of the "male" books), but neither do I pretend that mine is an authoritative book. I simply offer an appraisal of some of the more helpful literature together with a rather pragmatic classification of sexual behaviour, based mainly on what is known about the effectiveness of existing therapies. Like the earlier writers, I agree that there are three main categories, but mine are:

i)   coercive sex crimes which involve male-female power relationships, e.g. the sexual abuse of women, children and relatively powerless men;

ii) variant sexual behaviour which involves both men and women, about which we know little - other than that it is highly resistant to change, e.g. transsexualism, transvestism, homosexuality; and

iii) variant sexual behaviour which affects men only, seems to indicate a form of stunted heterosexuality and is open to change, e.g. voyeurism, exhibitionism, fetishism, transvestism, paedophilia.

I also offer a section on sexual dysfunction and an outline of the various popular therapies, together with some conclusions. These latter try to explain why transvestism and paedophilia sit uneasily in my classification and I suggest that it is social pressures on men which often pushes them towards behaviours which either cause them to abuse weaker people or find expression in unusual sexual behaviour. The people I think probably know most about sexual behaviour are the media agony aunts but, until this "data" is considered as valid as that of Kinsey (1948, 1953) and Masters and Johnson (1966, 1970), I offer this small book.

References

Beach, F. A. (1977). *Human Sexuality in Four Perspectives.*
John Hopkins Press.

Crolley, T. and Paley, J. (1982). 'Sexual Problems and the Probation
Service' *Probation Journal.* Vol 29, No4, pp133-137.

Davies, L. (1984). *Sex and the Social Worker.* Heinemann.

Gosselin, C. and Wilson, G. (1984). 'Fetishism and Sadomasochism'
in: *The Psychology of Sexual Diversity* (ed) Howell, L.
Basil Blackwell.

Hart, J. (1981). 'Social Workers and Paedopohiles: some dilemmas'
in: *Perspectives on Paedophilia* (ed) Taylor, B. Batsford Academic.

James, T. E. (1964). 'Law and the Sexual Offender' in:
The Pathology and Treatment of Sexual Deviation (ed) Rosen, I.
Oxford University Press.

Kinsey, A. C., Pomeroy, W. B. and Martin, C. E. (1948).
Sexual Behaviour in the Human Male. W. B. Saunders & Co.

Kinsey, A. C., Pomeroy, W. B. and Martin , C. E. & Gebhard, P.H.
(1953). *Sexual Behaviour in the Human Female.* W. B. Saunders

Masters, W. H. and Johnson, V. (1967). *The Human Sexual
Response.* Little, Brown Co.

Masters, W. H. and Johnson, V. (1970). *Human Sexual Inadequacy.*
Little, Brown Co.

Plummer, K. (1981) (ed). *The Making of the Modern Homosexual.*
Hutchinson.

Scott, P. D. (1964). 'Definition, Classification, Prognosis and
Treatment' in: *The Pathology and Treatment of Sexual Deviation*
(ed) Rosen, I. Oxford University Press.

Trimmer, E. (1978). *Basic Sexual Medicine.* Heinemann.

Chapter One

Coercive Sex Crimes

The single largest problem for social workers dealing with sex offenders who have coerced their victims stems from the fact that they are asked to deal with individual, aberrant males who are considered to have either been carried away on a lustful passion or have committed heinous crimes which are totally alien to the average man's nature. In reality, social workers find themselves dealing with fairly ordinary, heterosexual, married men who either have a high capacity for violence generally or who regularly misuse their power as head of the family. Although the effects of coerced sex are similar for the victims, the rape of women and children will be considered separately here - largely because the "facts" about rape have been challenged by the research earlier than the "facts" about child sexual abuse.

Sexual Abusers of Adults

Rapists have far more characteristics in common with the average violent criminal than with the average sex offender; burglary and drunkeness are more likely forerunners of sexual assault than voyeurism or making obscene phone calls (Trimmer 1978, Burgess et al 1978). For example, there are clear parallels between the patterns of rape and those of violent crimes. Studies show that:

> the majority of rapists have been drinking heavily,

> 60% of victims knew their assailant,

> 80% of victims were subjected to force, especially if they fought,

> 29% of cases involved weapons, usually a knife,

> 10% of cases involved robbery,

70% of rapists have convictions for non-sexual assault and robbery.

(Toner 1979, Wright 1980).

Thus, the recent case in which a vicar was battered with a cricket bat and his son's girlfriend raped during a burglary is fairly typical apart from the fact that it involved a group of men rather than an individual and one must assume that the public outcry which it inspired had more to do with it being a vicar who was attacked rather than a girl who was raped.

Also, the key factors involved in becoming a rape victim are neither age nor seductiveness as many people believe. As in mugging and burglary, vulnerability and accessibility of potential victims seem to be the prime factors (Katz & Mazur 1979). Rape is primarily an aggress-ive act out of which the rapist gets tremendous feelings of power rather than sexual satisfaction. Most rapists are not sexually frustrated men led on by teasing women; they are usually involved in a normal heterosexual relationship at the time of the offence. They are, however, usually men who have emotional difficulties in relationships and difficulty in asserting themselves with both men and women. It would be more helpful if social workers recognised the power elements in the offence rather than concentrating on the sexual elements as this would help to establish motivation and point to appropriate therapies (Geisner 1979).

Groth (1979), for example, found that using this basis, rapists fall into three main categories:

a)   *anger rape* - the aims here being to hurt and debase the victim to offset anger and resentment. Such rapes are usually impulsive, involving a high degree of force and little sexual gratification.

b)   *power rape* - this is the most common form of rape; sexuality becomes a means of compensating for inadequacy and it expresses mastery, control and capability. Rapists in this category commonly report masturbatory fantasies about sexual control and usually plan the rape with known victims which makes it seem to involve co-operation. Evidence from Rape Crisis Centres (1984) shows that this is the most under-reported form of rape, although a shift in attitudes in the police force and the setting up of special rape suites for victims has led to more victims reporting the assault.

c) *sadistic rape* - here the sexual transformation of anger and power means that anger becomes eroticised. Offenders usually find satisfaction in abusing, degrading and destroying the victim. It is always premeditated. I would consider the public response of castration for offenders to fall into this category which, I think, shows that women, too, are capable of expressing their power-lessness in terms of rape.

So, though we should be concentrating on the power elements of the behaviour - particularly the inability of rapists to express their powerlessness in any more acceptable way - I think social workers should be wary of viewing rape simply as a symptom of breakdown in male-female relationships and an abuse of male power. Although victims are mostly women, rapists are expressing their anger and resentment at the whole of society - they find it is equally hard to be a man among men as to be a man in relationships with women. They not only abuse their power over women but they challenge the power of all other men. For example, Peter Sutcliffe, the Yorkshire Ripper, was the most powerful man in the North of England for some consid-erable time. He not only had entire police forces running around after him but he also dictated the behaviour of all other men in the North. During his reign of terror, any one man on the streets at night was under suspicion and every family man had to escort the vulnerable members of his family on every evening trip, however trivial or short. Thus, Sutcliffe effectively disempowered men as well as women. It is hardly surprising, then, that the male psychiatrists who examined him declared him to be seriously insane. To have done otherwise would have been to acknowledge his male dominance.

Sexual Abusers of Children

Similarly, in the area of child sexual abuse, research shows that the behaviour is more indicative of a misuse of power than a simple sexual act. Trimmer (1978) regards incestuous fathers as rapists and Ward (1984) regards all males in power situations in families who sexually abuse children as rapists, and she considers this to include stepfather, uncles, cousins who stop the night, babysitters, etc. Despite some myths about children finding affection in incestuous relationships, the research shows that children are much more likely to be subjected to force and exploitation rather than seduction. As in the rape of adults, vulnerability (being too timid or young to protest) and accessibility seem to be the key factors in becoming a victim.

The problem of child sexual assault, like adult rape, is that the incidence is seriously underestimated, despite strong evidence to the contrary. It is not at all unusual. The Kinsey Report (1953) estimated that twenty-five percent of all women and a substantial proportion of all men experienced some form of sexual abuse in childhood and this figure is borne out by the subjective findings of incest crisis centres. As in rape of adults, the offenders are not unusual men. Certainly, they are not paedophiles who are usually shy of, or averse to, adult women.

Weinberg (1976) describes two typical forms of family dynamics implicated in incest: *endogamic* - family centred homes with affection-seeking, passive fathers; and *psychopathic* - indiscriminately promiscuous fathers. But as Ward (1984) points out, these sorts of fathers are actually very similar in that they both utterly dominate the family group:

> *Thus the two types of offenders, as described by*
> *researchers, are generally failures as men in the*
> *public world, and dictators of one sort or another*
> *within the private world of the family.*

Social workers, then, should consider the coercive sex offender within a wider context than individual, pathological, sexual behaviour. Many writers see the problem lying within male-female power positions and the exclusion of men from involvement with children. Peterson and Robson (1969), for example, say that the only predictable way that fathers show interest in their daughters is in an early and strong insistence that their girls conform to rigid stereotypes of femininity. Ward (1984) feels that men who betray trust cannot be forgiven and Herman (1982) feels that the answer lies in including men in the care and nurturing of children. However, although the behaviour is an expression of anger and resentment, and is directed at weaker members of society - women, children and frail men in male

18

institutions such as prisons and schools, it involves more than a need to re-align male-female and father-child relationships. It expresses a basic failure to cope in a male world and, despite the fact that almost a quarter of all men are expressing this failure, images of successful maleness persist. We need to examine how men generally defend themselves from the truth about the behaviour of rapists and their denial of the enormous pressures the male role places on men generally.

Men's Attitudes Towards Coercive Sex Offenders

Despite the fact that coerced sexual activity gives little sexual satisfaction to the perpetrators, and does an immense amount of damage to the victims, and despite the fact that evidence shows it to occur on an enormous scale, little is done about it. The recent spate of information on the subject has led to small improvements in police reception of victims, a spate of booklets on child abuse and a demand for longer prison sentences. We cannot lock up a quarter of the male population for periods of up to ten years each! The current reality is probably one in which there could be theoretically almost as many child sexual abusers amongst the prison officers as there are within the prison population.

The reasons for the massive denial of what our society is doing to its weaker members, the assailants as well as the victims, is not hard to find. Men find it very difficult to accept that a beast might lurk inside each and every one of them. Women and children rarely have to face this fear (they have so few opportunities for it to surface), but men are horrified at the idea that they too might not be caring, considerate and successful husbands and fathers. When students bring child sexual abuse cases for discussion in seminars, I find that many of the male students become upset and emotional. This is not unreasonable; they may find that their behaviour towards women and children will be misinterpreted. Davies (1984) deals with the residential social worker's dilemma extremely well in his book "Sex and the Social Worker" but a worker would need to be very secure in both his manhood and his professionalism not to feel uneasy.

A friend, recently exposed to the realities of educational programmes aimed at preventing child sexual abuse, commented in great distress:

"my niece (a teacher on the programme) *tells me that grandfathers do it too. Surely that can't be true?"* He could well imagine that brutish fathers or husbands might exist, but the notion that a grandfather might abuse the little child on his knee was something he found so repulsive and abhorrent that he could not accept it as a reality at all. When I suggested that abusing grandfathers had probably been abusing fathers and husbands too, and pointed out that it was an abuse of power rather than a sexual impulse, he felt much more comfortable. Secure in his role as a caring, egalitarian husband and successful businessman, he then knew that *he* could never become an abusing grandfather.

This intense uncomfortableness which men experience within themselves when they have to face up to facts about coercive sexual activity is the main reason why the problem remains hidden and the majority of crimes unreported. To save themselves from all becoming beasts, men redefine the problem. They ignore their own part in making some men so frustrated and so many people victims by emphasising the sexual elements of the crime. They define the parameters of the behaviour, they always give any benefit of doubt to men, they classify offences in terms of seriousness, they operate a rule of optimism and they blame victims and their mothers. They simply dissociate themselves from the behaviour as far as possible, but in a complex manner.

Firstly, in defining the parameters of the offence and emphasising the sexual elements, they ensure that legal definitions of crimes are carefully framed, thus keeping the number of "actual" offences in "proportion". Legal definitions of rape usually involve issues such as penile penetration and absence of consent, despite the fact that many rapists cannot manage "ordinary" intercourse and tend to demand oral sex (Toner 1979) and that victims do not make neat distinctions between the details of the rape. Even Gita Sereny (1984), in her sensitive book on child prostitution, says:

> *Twelve of the sixty-nine children had been sexually abused in childhood,* **though some only marginally** *(ie. not necessarily penetrated, by parents or relatives)".*

(Sereny 1984, my highlighting)

Tight legal definitions do no more than keep the numbers down (for details about police attitudes on these issues see, for example, the police introduction to the new police surgeons' booklet on the "sympathetic" handling of rape victims (McKay 1984)). Prosecutions and convictions are also kept artificially low by two methods. Firstly, the man is always given the benefit of the doubt, especially if the only other witness is a child (a catch 22 situation which has led to an MP "abusing" parliamentary privilege - and everyone debating the privilege rather than the frustration which gave rise to the MP in question "naming names"). Secondly, both victims and accused are allowed to remain anonymous. In the offenders' case, this is to protect all men against the slight chance of libel and in the victims' case to protect their good name and hide their shame. Absolute rubbish! Both should be named as in any other legal proceedings, apart from juveniles. Old ladies who are viciously mugged are always named and get floods of sympathy from the public. Why not the same for rape victims? Why should they have to hide their shame? They have been brutally attacked but the legal system defines them as having been defiled and dishonoured. Whose blushes are being saved - the victim's or her man's? The reality is that we are just a little more refined than the Indian families who used to murder their raped and defiled daughters.

We also try to keep the crime levels "in proportion" by trying to classify the seriousness of the offence. For example, a social worker, describing a child sexual abuse case to me recently, said: *"well, it was a stepfather, not a real father, so I suppose that is not so bad . . ."* Similarly, in prison, offenders develop a pecking order and are much more likely to beat up a man who sexually abuses strange women or children rather than one who abuses his "own" family - although the victims all perceive it as the same offence.

We are all guilty of the "rule of optimism" as firstly described in the literature on non-accidental injury (Dingwall et al 1983) and later given further credence by the Beckford Report (1985). We, none of us, men or women, really want to know about the truly horrible things which happen to some people and we willingly close our eyes. Again, Sereny (1984) castigates social workers for allowing an abusing father access at weekends to his child in care:

*What they didn't know - one wonders how they would
miss the tell-tale signs - was that when she was nine,
the father raped her, and from then on had intercourse
with her every weekend and all holidays*

but, at the same time, accepts a fifteen year old male prostitute's explanations for why he walked as though it hurt and sat down gingerly, as piles of nine years' duration. She fails totally to link this with the nine years since the boy was anally and painfully raped by his eighteen year old cousin staying overnight. It is, quite simply, easier *not* to see what is happening and then we don't have to do anything about it. If we keep the numbers down and say some offences are more serious than others, we can be punitive with a few and ignore the rest. This denies the reality of the experience for the victim and denies the offender a chance of any meaningful therapy.

And, of course, we can always pretend that the man had nothing to do with the offence at all. We can always say that the victim was the intitiator or willing accomplice. Is real power so shaky a thing that we have to pretend that the relatively powerless are all experts in exercising subtle, covert control? Or is it preferable to think that offenders are easily tempted to stray . . .? Child sexual abusers often accuse the children of being seductive or it being for the child's own good; "*it were better that she learnt from me than them no-good lads*" was what one incestuous father said to me about his fifteen year old daughter's pregnancy. And little could I do about the statement as I spent the next half hour trying to prevent my male colleague from murdering the man there and then. So it went unchallenged.

We know that pubescent children can flaunt their new found sexual attributes and we believe that they may be seductive. But most children are abused well before puberty (Koblinski and Behana 1984) and Howell's (1979) careful research into child victims shows that the children were largely unloved and unsupervised, looking for affection, not sex. Similarly, adult rape victims are commonly thought to have provoked some redblooded, lustful man by their teasing, coquettish behaviour. This is not merely a standard defence lawyer's plea (some of the worst rapists of all, according to victims) but a very typical male attitude as recent research corroborates. Thornton and Ryckman (1983) asked sixty-four males and sixty female students to read an account of a sexual assault and then answer questions about their attitudes towards the victim. Each account had a photograph of either an attractive or an unattractive nineteen year old attached to it. The results showed that not only were the men more likely than women to think that the rape victims were personally responsible for what happened to them but they also thought that the unattractive girls were generally more responsible for getting raped than the good looking ones! Plain, powerless people take note - you are not worth anything.

Failing all else, we can always blame mothers. And here, I am not referring simply to traditional male reactions. Mother blaming is a popular pastime with most social workers. Firstly, mothers are an easy target for social workers - they are most likely to be at home during the day when social workers prefer to call, therefore preventing the necessity of doing an evening visit. Secondly, they usually take on responsibility for the behaviour of the family, what Ward (1984) refers to as the feminine role model which *"establishes motherhood as the moral and behavioural arbiter of everyone else in the family. And therefore the keeper of secrets"*. In addition, fathers willingly opt out; a good Yorkshire husband is considered one who hands over his wage packet and helps with the washing up. Fathers not infrequently tell social workers at the door: *"I'm sorry, there's no one in"*.

Working *on* mothers for all social ills is therefore often standard social work practice, although now, some social workers are talking about working *with* mothers for a change (see, for example, Hale 1984). However, the willing acceptance of social workers to blame mothers, particularly in child sexual abuse cases, where they are often accused of being frigid, hostile, rejecting and saboteurs of therapy (Fawcett 1986), lies mainly in the legacy of Freud and his male-biased psychology of human development, which is the theoretical underpinning of much traditional psychosocial casework. There are several telling critiques of Freudian theory (Rorbaugh 1981, Gilligan 1982) but perhaps Ward's (1984) analysis is the most compelling. She argues that Freud was so shocked himself by women's "sexual shock" that he had to devise the oedipal/electra complex. Thus, by burying reality into women's subconsciousness and maintaining that all women fantasise about sexual relationships with their fathers, he gave scientific credence to the myths that children "make it up" and "women ask for it". Ward argues then that men can erect images about coercive sexual encounters which enable society to forgive and forget the offender (a man), to bind and blame mothers (all women), and to label and libel daughters (all children) as manipulative and liars.

Most social workers will recognise these stereotypes as they struggle to work with families in which the man appears weak and ineffectual, the mother dominant and difficult and the children disruptive and ambivalent. They need to recognise that these families reflect societal attitudes concerned with avoiding reality. Unless they reach out to the man's failure and the victim's powerlessness, they cannot start to begin effective therapy. I would caution, though, against an entirely feminist perspective; simply blaming men or trying to involve them more fully in families in an egalitarian way is not sufficient. It is powerlessness within the modern world which is most central. Whilst it is men mainly who batter their wives, rape women, abuse children and sexually harass women at work, this is not necessarily sex-specific behaviour. I strongly suspect that women in power may well have the potential to abuse it, and the sexual way is the quickest and most humiliating way. I know that I, as a fairly powerful woman at work, have come close to sexual harassment of younger male colleagues when I have felt particularly annoyed and I am not proud of it.

These issues of powerfulness, success, competency, security and self esteem, are I suspect the key issues for social workers. If they are avoided and instead the sexual components of the offence are concentrated upon, then many offenders will not be effectively helped to change their coping mechanisms. Social workers need to like themselves and feel secure in themselves if they are to help their offending clients to like themselves and respect others.

The Effects of Sexual Assault on Victims

With child sexual abuse currently so much in the headlines, many social workers are afraid that "jumping on the bandwagon" and becoming heavily interventionist may be more harmful to victims than maintaining the status quo by doing nothing. After all, if it is happening on such a large scale, then many people seem to have survived it quite well. Should we dig up old hurts, rape the victim a second time, break up more families, incarcerate more men, and put more children into care? For social workers, these dilemmas often obscure the primary effects of the assault and interventions often seem to create secondary effects - as is illustrated by the following case example:

> At fifteen, Sharon Green told a school teacher that she was being sexually abused by her father. The shocked teacher informed the police and social services. She could not think fast enough on her feet to talk to Sharon about what the assault meant to her. Sharon went straight into care on a place of safety order and was placed with newly registered foster parents, who hadn't a clue about child sexual abuse. No doubt they were alarmed that their first foster child was a sexually experienced teenager. If she had lost a parent rather than her innocence they might have found it easier to cope. Soon Sharon was with a second foster family and very quickly in a children's home.
>
> Meanwhile, Sharon's family protested father's innocence. "Children don't make these things up", said the social worker. The family said Sharon was just saying it because she couldn't get her own way with father (the start of the labelling process for the daughter) and that she had that sort of knowledge because her grandfather had sexually abused her two years ago. They had done nothing then, apart from keeping grandfather away (the start of the secret?), although he had since been convicted of sexually assaulting other children.
>
> This family "defence" of father indicated that he was probably abused himself as a child and it is likely that he would become an abusing father in turn (Kempe and Henry 1977). Indeed, it transpired that he had a spent conviction for the rape of a juvenile some years previously. But he is innocent, protests mother. (As Fawcett 1986, comments: *"incest is a symptom of serious dysfunction within the family unit, but one which acts at the same time as a means of holding the family together by keeping the incest a secret"*). Father says he would agree to therapy but it would imply guilt - so he won't. A reasonable man, thinks the social worker, but mother is very difficult and dominant.
>
> Meanwhile Mrs Green is visiting Sharon in the children's home. She is ambivalent, hostile and rejecting of Sharon, who is accused of breaking up the family. Sharon becomes very withdrawn and difficult to deal with. Peters (1976) argues that the child's withdrawal under these pressures is such that social workers cannot evaluate the child. Here they evaluate her as manipulative and difficult and mother as a problem. Everyone seems to have forgotten that Mr Green is accused of the offence and, in all probability, has been offending for years.

Sharon withdraws her allegations and, when a further interim care order is made, says that she wants to go home. What should the social worker do? If a full care order is made, Sharon will probably abscond until she ends up in secure accommodation. If a supervision order is made, the family might co-operate. However, the social worker is not entirely happy about the teenager brothers' attitude. They reject and blame Sharon but they seem rather flirty and familiar with Mrs Green ...

The dilemma for the social worker is that care does not seem a very good option for Sharon, so a return home is seriously considered. However, it should not be. The research shows very clearly that offenders continue to offend and that victims suffer serious physical, emotional and social consequences. They suffer a betrayal of innocence and carry a huge burden of guilt, shame and secret-keeping. They learn that they are worthless, that no one can, or will, help them and they develop a negative self image, long-term guilt, mistrust of men (and all authority) and sexual dysfunction (Forward and Buck 1978, Armstrong 1978). Should Sharon be subjected to this or should social workers shout long and hard for adequate care facilities for abused children - and rape victims? The value of hostels for battered wives is now accepted; why not something similar for the victims of sexual abuse? Adult rape victims suffer similar sorts of effects, especially to their feelings of confidence and self worth.

There are other victims in this scenario. Sharon's mother is also a victim. She has committed no crime but is considered a failure as a wife and mother. She is placed in a situation where she has to choose her husband and reject her daughter and she is certain to be blamed. Most writers in the field of the sexual abuse of children consider the breakdown of the mother-daughter relationship as fairly typical of these situations and blame family power structures. However, other people too can suffer from this form of secondary assault and blame for failing to save the vulnerable family member. Trimmer (1978) and FulgateWoods (1977) both comment on the need for counselling of the husband or boyfriend of a rape victim as they, too, often show ambivalence and inability to help the rape victim effectively.

Thus it seems that a victim's most likely source of emotional help, a mother or husband, is also disabled by the assault and prevented from taking up their natural roles by virtue of their own feelings of shame, guilt and failure. Mothers feel that they have failed in their sex role if their husbands abuse their children; husbands feel that they have failed in their sex role by not keeping their wife safe from external assault. So, at a time when they most desperately need support, sympathy, reassurance and help, the sexually abused child or adult is a source of embarrassment and shame to other family members. The victim is totally isolated. And when they tell someone, what does that person do? Usually they are shocked, then they send for the fire brigade, then they try to withdraw. No wonder most victims keep quiet. But, if you are a social worker and you are dealing with a sexually abused person, you should do something. You should prevent it happening again and you should try to repair the damage.

What can social workers do?

Social workers should be able to deal with the hurt, guilt and shame which their clients are experiencing. However, often their own feelings of shock get in the way and they don't always take in the full implications of what is happening. Thus, their responses are often stilted at best and denying at worst - abused children typically report the offence several times before they are believed. Perhaps all social workers should practice receiving shocking information so that they can be more confident about their response. After all, most social workers are prepared to support bereaved, grieving and hurt clients, so why should they be any less able in this area?

A "dry run" is also important so that social workers can handle the information sensitively. Many abused people complain of secondary assault by professionals - adults talk about court appearances as a second rape and children complain that adults often want them to repeat the details too often. They quite rightly suspect adults of a certain prurience. The sordid details are only relevant to the ridiculous legal classification system of offences; the victim needs help with the emotional aspects of the case, the assault on their privacy, esteem and worth. I think it would be better if the offences were all classified as grievous bodily harm and, although this is unlikely to happen, it would be a better starting point for social work efforts than sexual details. Unless the victim needs reassurance about future sexual functioning, then there is little need to dwell on them.

Because of the heavy burden of guilt and shame involved, social workers need to be able to use a wide range of communication skills. Crisis centres are extremely effective at breaking through resistance to talk about the assault and ventilation certainly seems helpful as was well illustrated on television recently when four American rape victims met four rapists. Whenever possible, group discussions are helpful as victims invariably feel more comfortable about disclosures within an understanding group situation. Where the counselling must be on an individual basis, play therapy (particularly using anatomically correct dolls) seems to be the most effective method (Bannister 1985). Play therapy was originally devised as a way of getting through to very withdrawn children or with young children unable to express the relevant concepts verbally, but Tucker (1985) cautions against "leading" children too much in doll play. Baker (1986) suggests that social workers should be familiar with the dolls before using them with children; "they should 'play' with them". Interestingly, it is not only small children who benefit from play therapy; a mother's group run by the NSPCC regularly uses the children's toys, expressing their anger at the men dolls and rearranging the doll's house; a children's home in Lancashire has found messy play, plasticene, sand, mud, etc., extremely effective with difficult adolescents. A "consumer guide"to books, videos, etc., available for this area of work, is appended to Chapter Three.

Throughout the helping process, social workers need to be very aware of themselves as models of authority and adulthood to the victim. A sexually abused person does not feel safe and the social workers have to be able to demonstrate that they can protect the victim from further assault. And assault is not merely sexual abuse; it is assault and power from authority figures. Female social workers need to be aware of themselves as female role models - they really do need to show the victim that women can be in control of their destinies and be appropriately assertive. Male social workers have to tread a delicate path between being "just another man" and a superior father. These are difficult issues for social workers but not really different from the role problems of any residential social worker in child care. The most difficult issue for social workers is that they are often powerless themselves within their own organisations.

The confident social worker can do much to help victims beyond counselling aimed at the specific assault. They can build self esteem, teach assertiveness and empower abused people. Even at a simple level, Sandford (1980) says that, by teaching a child to say "no" and by getting the father to repeat this, then the father's chance of successfully victimising his children has been removed. All the experts stress the importance of working to improve the mother-daughter bond in cases of child sexual abuse and the husband-wife bond in cases of adult sexual abuse. Ward (1984) says:

> The welfare system needs, most of all, to change its primary focus from that of family "welder" (trying to get the family back together at all costs), to that of care and protection for the daughter and understanding for the mother.

Herman (1982), who recommends working with men to improve their relationships with women and children, cautions:

> Men cannot be expected to overcome their abusive tendencies or to develop their nurturant capacities overnight, and it makes no sense to expose children to the unsupervised care of men whose interests in them may be ambivalent at best, and perverse at worst.

Summary

The social work task with offenders and victims in sexual abuse is an enormous one as it involves so many people and such entrenched attitudes. However, we cannot really accept that so many people are raped and degraded and that so many men feel such failures that they need to rape and degrade others. In so far as this chapter is about sex at all, it is about our own feelings about sex. The social work task in this area is a familiar and central one - it is about helping people to discover their own strengths and use them, facilitating growth and coping, encouraging worth and self esteem, repairing hurt and, most difficult of all, demanding adequate care resources for the safety and protection of victims.

References

A Child in Trust: The Report of the Panel of Inquiry into the Circumstances Surrounding the Death of Jasmine Beckford (1985). Presented to Brent Borough Council and to Brent Health Authority by Members of the Panel of Inquiry. London Borough of Brent.

Armstrong, L. (1978). *Kiss Daddy Goodnight.* Pocket Books.

Baker, A. (1986). 'The Power of Play'. *Community Care.* Jan 23, pp14-16.

Bannister, A. (1985). 'Monster-Man Has Gone'. *Community Care.* Nov 28, pp20-21.

Burgess, A. W., Groth, A. N., Holmstron, L. L. & Sgroi, S. M. (1978). *Sexual Assault of Children and Adolescents.* Lexington Books.

Davies, L. (1984). *Sex and the Social Worker.* Heinemann.

Dingwall, R., Eckalaar, J. & Murray, T. (1983). *The Protection of Children: State Intervention and their Implications.* HMSO.

Fawcett, J. (1986). 'Mothers and Daughters'. *Community Care.* February 27, pp16-18.

Forward, S. & Buck, J. C. (1978). *Betrayal of Innocence.* Penguin.

FulgateWoods, N. (1977). *Human Sexuality in Health and Illness.* C. V. Moseby Co.

Geisner, R. (1979). *Hidden Victims - the Sexual Abuse of Children.* Beacon Press.

Gilligan, C. (1982). *In a Different Voice.* Harvard University Press.

Groth, A. N. (1979). *Men Who Rape.* Plenum Press.

Hale, J. (1984). 'Feminism and Social Work Practice' in: *The Political Dimensions of Social Work* (eds) Jordan, B. & Parton, N. Basil Blackwell.

Herman, J. (1982). *Father-Daughter Incest.* Harvard University Press.

Katz, S. & Mazur, K. A. (1979). *Understanding the Rape Victim.* J Wiley.

Kempe, C. & Henry, M. D. (1977). *Sexual Abuse: Another Hidden Pediatric Problem.* Paper presented at the annual meeting of America's Academy of Pediatrics. New York City. November.

Kinsey, A. C., Pomerory, W. B., Martin, C. E. & Gebhard, P. H. (1953). *Sexual Behaviour in the Human Female.* W. B. Saunders & Co.

Koblinsky, S. & Behana, N. (1984). 'Child Sexual Abuse: the educators role in prevention, detection and intervention'. *Young Children.* September.

McKay, W. D. S. (ed) (1984). *The New Police Surgeon: Rape.* Published by the Association of Public Surgeons of Great Britain: Creaton House, Creaton, Northampton, NN6 8ND, in association with the W. G. Johnson Memorial Trust Fund.

Peterson, F. A. & Robson, K. S. (1969). 'Fathers Participation in Infancy'. *American Journal of Orthopsychiatry.* 39, 466-472.

Peters, J. (1976). 'Children who are victims of sexual assaults and the psychology of offenders'. *American Journal of Psychotherapy.* 30, p417.

Rohrbaugh, J. B. (1981). *Woman: Psychology's Puzzle.* Abacus.

Sandford, L. (1980). *The Silent Children: A Parent's Guide to the Prevention of Child Sexual Abuse.* Doubleday Anchor Press.

Sereny, G. (1984). *The Invisible Children.* Pan Books.

The London Rape Crisis Centre (1984). *Sexual Violence: the reality for women.* The Women's Press.

Thornton, B. & Ryckman, R. (1983). 'The Influence of a Rape Victim's Physical Attractiveness on Observers' Attributions of Responsibility'. *Human Relations.* 36, 6, p549.

Toner, B. (1979). *The Facts of Rape.* Hutchinson.

Trimmer, E. (1978). *Basic Sexual Medicine.* Heinemann.

Tucker, N. (1985). 'A Panic Over Child Abuse'. *New Society,* 18 Oct.

Ward, E. (1984). *Father-Daughter Rape.* The Women's Press.

Weinberg, S. K. (1976). *Incest Behaviour.* Citadel Press (Revised Edition)

Wright, R. (1980). 'The English Rapist'. *New Society,* 17 July.

Chapter Two

Gender Disorders

This chapter is concerned with my second classification, variant sexual behaviour which is highly resistant to change. I shall discuss people whose sexual behaviour does not accord with their biological sex in the way we would expect it to and who resist very strongly any attempts to change their sexual feelings, attitudes and behaviour despite overt societal disapproval. Most people whose sexual behaviour does not accord with accepted norms tend to be very secretive in that they either practice the behaviour in private or, if an offence is involved, try to avoid detection. However, transsexuals, transvestites and homosexuals, although they may begin secretly, usually progress to a point where they are making a public statement about their sexuality. Because their behaviour seems so very odd to most of us, yet not necessarily perverse, there have been many attempts to explain their behaviour in terms of gender disorder.

On a simple level, this seems an entirely convincing explanation. Oakley (1972) says that sex is a biological norm and gender is a psychological and cultural norm. Sex is determined at birth (and entered unalterably into birth certificates) but gender is open to many influences. For example, there are psychosexual developmental issues (Erikson 1948), social learning influences of differential reinforcements, imitation, identification and modelling (Bandura & Walters 1969), cognitive elements (Piaget 1965, Kohlberg 1969), hormonal, ethological and anthropological influences (Lee & Stewart 1976) and power structures (Chetwynd & Hartnett 1978, Oakley 1972). If so many factors can influence our perceptions of masculinity and femininity, then it seems quite reasonable that several people will vary from their biological sex, ultimately choosing a partner from the same biological sex or trying to change their bodies to fit their gender identities.

But these explanations are too general and too contentious to be of much help in either understanding or helping people we label as suffering from a gender disorder. In the first place, the starting point of this explanation is that biological sex is a fixed, irreducible fact and this is not the case. Not only are mistakes sometimes made in the determination of sex at birth, but the ratio of male and female births is affected by non-biological factors. For example, there is a primary sex ratio in that more females are conceived than males and a secondary sex ratio in that more males are born than females. And this ratio is further affected by such diverse factors as blood groups, artificial insemination, paternal employment, seasons and rainwater (McFarlane & Mugford 1984).

Secondly, there is little theoretical consensus about how the various influences outlined above interact in gender acquisition; so we don't know which are the important factors. Thirdly, there is little agreement on how much weight we should give to notions of gender role and gender identity in our explanations of gender disorder. Gender identity is privately experienced - it is what one thinks one is - and gender role is the public manifestation of identity. Thus, Money (1982) argues:

> *The role (and hence the identity) comprises everything that one says or does to manifest oneself as masculine, feminine or androgynous.*

And he focuses, therefore, mainly on gender role in his explanation of gender disorders, or to use his term, dysphoria (an "unbalance" of gender). He argues that several gender role transpositions occur (Money, 1973):

	Total	Partial	Optional
Episodic	transvestism	bisexualism	recreational
Chronic	transsexualism	homosexual	elective

Brierley (1984), on the other hand, argues that this model depends too much on the influences of social learning and "fixes" gender role at too early a stage in development. While he accepts that biological and learning factors are implicated, he argues that one must try to account for the obvious blurring between transsexualism, transvestism and fetishism which occurs well into adulthood. He would give more weight to the notion of gender identity and finds personal construct theory more helpful in understanding variant behaviour, the implication being that we should not conceptualise sexual variations as discrete entities.

I find Brierley's arguments attractive but feel that, from a social work point of view, we must accept that people are labelled and that we find it easier to deal with people if we can categorise them. Therefore I will discuss gender disorders as discrete entities in this chapter in so far as many transsexuals, transvestites and homosexuals who come to the attention of social workers will have gender identities and roles which are relatively stable and compatible. However, accepting Brierley's point about gender identity being not necessarily fixed early on in life, I am quite happy to include transvestism in the section on fetishism too. Equally, distinctions made in this book between the serious sexual assaulter of children and the sad paedophile will not always be clear. All I think can be said with any certainty in this chapter is that we really don't know very much about gender disorders and the social worker's role in this area is a very limited one.

Transsexualism

What is it?

Transsexualism is the term used to describe men and women who believe that they have been assigned the wrong sex and who wish to correct the "error" by means of dress, hormone treatment and, sometimes, radical sex realignment surgery. So, although the actual numbers of transsexuals is quite small (Hoenig and Kenna, 1974), they constitute a large problem for medical services simply because biological sex cannot be fundamentally changed. They pose particular problems for social workers when their requests for surgery are turned down.

Transsexualism is often confused with transvestism and/or homosexuality although it has quite specific features. The confusion arises partly from societal attitudes - if a man has a "sex change" operation and, considering himself to be a woman, lives with a man, is he to be considered homosexual? Green (1981) refers to this as "expressing psychical heterosexuality and anatomical homosexuality". Confusion also arises because the individuals themselves often follow a career pattern of homosexuality to transvestism or female impersonation and then to transsexualism. However, transsexuals are neither transvestites nor homosexuals in their own minds; they are simply people who have felt trapped in the wrong body since early childhood and who wish to put matters right.

Where a social worker is in doubt about a cross-dressing client's orientation, he or she can sometimes get a hint from the female name assumed. Brierley (1979) found that male-to-female transsexuals usually choose a solidly female name for themselves - often one ending in an "a", such as Julia or Nichola. Susan and Caroline were also found to be popular. Transvestites, on the other hand, tend to choose conventionally pretty names, such as Julie and Rosemary. This is probably because the transsexual feels fairly comfortable with his feminine gender identity and feminine role and does not seek a conversion operation in order to escape masculine demands but rather to complete the process of becoming a woman (Buhrich 1986). However, the feminine gender identity tends to be a stereotyped one and I always feel that male-to-female conversion operations might not be so popular if the end product involved small beasts, large hips and hefty thighs. Much less is known about female-to-male transsexuals, the main study of this subject being so Freudian in orientation that many possible theoretical issues are not discussed (Lothstein 1983).

Quite simply, we do not really know what makes transsexuals behave in the way they do. What we do know is that they tend to pursue at least partial sex realignment therapy in an obsessive way and that,if refused treatment under the health service, are likely to travel to other countries for surgery often under hazardous physical conditions. Because of this, treatment is usually offered, but only after the transsexual has "proved" him/herself by living as a member of the opposite sex for some considerable time.

Hormone Treatment

A major problem for transsexuals, glossed over by them in an obsessive and urgent desire for a sex change, but a constant worry to their doctors, are the side-effects of hormone treatment. The suppression of facial and chest hair growth and the enlargement of breasts involves the use of large doses of feminising hormones as well as prolonged electrolysis. Large doses of oestrogens can precipitate thrombosis and breast carcinoma and should not be prescribed for people with severe hypertension, diabetes, obesity, heavy smoking habits or a history of breast carcinoma (Goodman 1982). Baldness, severe tiredness and thyrotoxicosis have also been reported in transsexuals undergoing hormone treatment (Dewhurst & Underhill 1979) and it is not always appreciated that the depth of a man's voice is unaffected by hormones and that some men continue to have at least partial erections despite a prolonged course of female hormones (Buhrich 1986). For women taking male hormones, the side-effects are equally severe, causing profound acne, sterility, an increased libido and an irreversible deepening of the voice. Hormone treatment has to be maintained throughout life, increasing the risk of liver tumours and not contributing greatly to any marked virilisation (Lothstein 1983).

Surgery

Sex realignment is not without its hazards either. It is easier for men who can have their genital organs removed and artificial vaginas constructed. However, many artifical vaginas become dry and painful and cannot contribute to sexual intercourse pleasure. For women, the problems of surgery are acute as it is impossible to create a functioning penis. Phalloplasty involves multiple operations and extensive surgical procedures which often cause enormous bladder problems. Lothstein (1983) reports that many female-to-male transsexuals settle for breast surgery so that they can walk about in public bare chested but this is not always satisfactory as the nipples have to be removed and regrafted, not always taking and often causing extensive scarring.

Even with "good" surgical results the operation is cosmetic at best rather than fundamental and there still remain problems of sexual ambiguity. These even occur during surgery as the surgeon has to decide on which ward the patient should be sited. One surgeon transfers patients after the operation to the ward of the sex types being created artificially. Also, after sex realignment surgery, the transsexual finds that he has a vagina but cannot menstruate or bear children or that she has a penis which will not ejaculate. Whilst national insurance cards, passports and medical cards can be obtained in the new sex, birth certificates cannot be changed and marriage is not permitted.

The immediate effects of therapy are good, with transsexuals reporting that they feel much better (Green 1981). However the limitations of therapy to effect a fundamental sex change begin to take their toll and the long-term results for transsexuals are not particularly good. The artifical mechanisms do not withstand wear and tear well and long-term follow-up at John Hopkins University found that many transsexuals become depressed and despairing as they realise that the change is incomplete. Also, post-operatively, the transsexuals' employment prospects do not improve (Mayer & Reters 1979) although many find employment as female impersonators.

The Social Work Role

The role of the social worker in this area is a limited one, mainly because transsexuals do not want their behaviour changing at all. There do not seem to be any reported cases of transsexuals becoming reconciled to their biological sex and it is probably better if a social worker refers a pre-treatment transsexual to one of the two self-help organisations, the Beaumont Society and SHAFT (the Self-help Association of Transsexuals). However, there is a social work task which often gets neglected at this point, namely the relatives of transsexuals. Whilst everyone is concentrating on the transsexual (an interesting case to anyone, even those who have no prurience at all), the relatives are often ignored and left alone with their feelings of failure and worries about their own gender identity. Buhrich (1986) reports that, whilst sisters may be sympathetic, fathers and brothers remain at best unenthusiastic. Having described at length in the previous chapter the problems for men "being men" in our society, I think it would be insensitive of a social worker to fail to offer some sort of counselling and support for a transsexual's family; after all, it is hardly the sort of problem they can discuss with friends in ordinary company.

Also, there is a role for social workers at a later stage in therapy. A tall, heavily-built man with a very deep voice will not be able to pass as a woman, even after treatment, and such people are likely to be refused surgery, especially if they seem to be at all unstable. These people may well end up in hospital following suicide and self-castration attempts and there have been suicide attempts following surgery (Randall 1971). Equally likely is the need for social work involvement with depressed transsexuals who have finally realised that they can never change biological sex, and these post-therapy transsexuals may well be ill people as a result of the therapy.

All in all, social work involvement means dealing with people who may well have suffered pain, anguish, mutilation and long-term iatrogenic illness, all to little success. The social work task is difficult because transsexuals want the impossible and cannot be persuaded other-wise. Also, we know so little about the causes of the condition, despite prestigious writers still daring to be dogmatic; for example, Kolodny, Masters and Johnson (1979) still feel confident enough to say *"It is important to remember that transsexualism is an illness, rather than a normal expression of human sexuality"*. I find I can make no really constructive suggestions, apart perhaps from pointing out that social workers are skilled at sustaining the desperate, the depressed and the trapped members of society. As social workers, you can offer support, sympathy and acceptance.

Transvestism

What is it?

Social workers often get very confused about what actually constitutes transvestism because the main feature of the condition involves cross-dressing and cross-dressing is extremely common behaviour in a wide range of circumstances. We have a long legacy of cross-dressing in entertainment, e.g. the traditional pantomine, and at fancy dress parties. Female impersonators are extremely common although male impersonators are rather more rare. Most people cross-dress at some times in their lives and, as long as it is short-lived or obviously "pretend" behaviour, then it is considered perfectly socially acceptable. The socially acceptable nature of the behaviour is signified by the grotesqueness of the impersonation; features are exaggerated but the real sex of the impersonator is rarely in question.

Some people cross-dress more seriously, and less socially acceptable, for reasons other than transvestism. For example, some homosexual prostitutes cross-dress for business and transsexuals cross-dress in the period immediately prior to sex realignment therapy. Apart from the last instance, no one cross-dressing would transcend male and female demarcations by using the "wrong" public lavatory. All these situations seem to confuse the social worker from working out who is actually transvestite; this confusion affects the advice they give to wives worried about their husbands' behaviour or decisions made about adolescent boys in children's homes - should their "dressing up" be taken seriously or is it a passing phase?

For the purposes of this section, transvestism is considered to be a persistent condition in which heterosexual men cross-dress in certain clearly defined ways. It is a form of behaviour which is highly resistant to traditional therapeutic interventions and which increases rather than decreases in intensity. Transvestism involves a bipolarity of gender role-taking in which there is a relatively stable feminine gender persona, in the context of a desire to preserve male hetero-sexuality and this is observed in cross-dressing. Money (1976) has referred to transvestism as "two wardrobes, two personalities and two names".

The two personalities are typically stereotyped with the male one tending to be successful, forceful and macho whilst the feminine one is soft and giggly. Transvestites are not homosexual and do not engage in sexual activity whilst cross-dressing; this is reserved for the male role-taking. As mentioned earlier, transvestites usually choose a pretty name for their female self and Brierley's extensive study (1979) found that transvestites often have the following features in common:

> an interest in constriction, wearing very tight corsets
> to achieve a slender, feminine figure;

> an obsessive interest in details of dress, such as
> intricate frills and rows of tiny buttons;

> a tendency to write about the ecstasy experience in
> cross-dressing and to subscribe to magazines catering
> for transvestite writings; and

> a tendency to give a well-rehearsed, selective personal
> history about the onset of transvestism.

Despite the well-rehearesed histories (not dissimilar to transsexuals' accounts of early childhood anguish), the behaviour seems to begin in puberty. Since in the early stages there are elements of fetishism, it could well be seen as a problem arising out of achieving a male identity and living up to a macho role. Stoller (1978) gives a basically Freudian interpretation of the origins of transvestism. He suggests that it arises from a fear of women's strength and that many transvestites have suffered humiliating experiences as young boys, being dressed in women's clothes and ridiculed. He suggests that the transvestite resolves his conflict of heterosexual needs (wanting women) with the fear of women by cross-dressing (identifying with women):

Each of these conflicts is solved by perversion;
beneath the women's clothes and the appearance
of being female (no penis), the transvestite has secretly
triumphed. His penis is still there and functioning, more
it is really there, triumphantly erect, victoriously male.

Hmm...; yes, to my mind another silly male explanation - phallocentric and unhelpful. My main reason for disregarding the festishistic elements of transvestism and its adolescent origins is that research shows that erotic elements and excitement about secretly cross-dressing disappear as transvestism continues. Psychoanalysis and psychotherapy, based on explanations such as Stroller's have proved remarkably ineffectual in changing the behaviour at all (Williams 1977). The Brierley study (1979), in fact, shows that, although there has been some marginal success in giving transvestites social skills training in the male role, at least seventy percent of all transvestites are far more interested in developing their female self than their male self. The behaviour seems to me to begin with problems in the male role which are gradually resolved by increasing the amount of female role-taking. The early behaviour involving constriction and details of dress reminds me more of my adolescent daughter at fourteen than of any peculiar sexual perversion. As older transvestites seem to settle down into middle-aged female role behaviour, especially where their wives are willing for them to cross dress at home, it seems to be that they have hit upon a very neat way of avoiding the pressures of the male role without losing any of the advantages.

What can social workers do?

The short answer is very little, especially as the Beaumont Society is very supportive. Where a transvestite waits until his children have left home and where his wife approves of his open cross-dressing or permits it within the home, then there seems to be no reason to do anything at all. However, the development of transvestism along a career path of marriage and heterosexual activity, combined with secret cross-dressing is very distressing for a number of wives. To have married a "macho" man and then find him wearing your clothes is bewildering and a severe blow to feminine self esteem. Wives report that their husbands' involvement in the Beaumont Society may well help the men but it alienates them from their wives who are offered no support (Prince 1967).

So the social worker may well become involved with the effects of transvestism on marriages, particularly those social workers involved in marital and divorce counselling. Again, this is not the sort of situation which a woman can discuss with her friends, so she is likely to be extremely isolated, vulnerable and lacking in self esteem. She is likely to feel a sexual failure and will need long-term support if she is to stay with her husband and thoughtful counselling if she wishes to divorce him. She is likely to be worried too about the sexual orientation of her children and may well need long-term support until her children are safely launched. As I have suggested earlier, social workers would do well to practise receiving shocking information so that they can receive clients' confidences and fears about what seems very bizarre to them, without appearing revolted or shocked themselves. What many women do suffer from is isolation; that theirs is not a rare problem has been borne out by the fact that, following lectures on transvestism, I have been the recipient of "secrets" on several occasions. To include case examples would be to risk breaching confidentiality but, as one student said, "I've wanted to tell someone for ages but I was too ashamed. I thought it must be because of me."

Homosexuality

What is it?

Because the main focus has been on male rather than female homo-sexuality and because most of the early research used emotionally disturbed or convicted subjects, several confusions about the nature of homosexuality are widespread. Particularly common is a tendency to equate homosexuality with paedophilia and, even today, social workers still try to "treat" homosexuals. Homosexuality is, quite simply, the preference for a sexual partner of the same sex.

There are numerous theories propounded as explanations for this sexual orientation, the most common being basically Freudian ones involving notions of inadequate oedipal development with weak fathers and dominant mothers in the case of male homosexuality (for an overview, see Kline 1972), and fear of mutilation via pregnancy in the case of female homosexuality (Jones 1927). Other theories range from biological to social learning and cultural influences (Plummer 1981), with the most sexist explanation coming from a male homosexual who suggests that homosexuality is functional for species survival as it prevents men from becoming bored with women (Tripp 1977). You will have noticed by now that women just can't win - when defined by men we are always dominant, or weak, or manipul-ative, or powerful, or boring!

A recent review of the "scientific" evidence (Feldman 1984) suggests two groups of homosexuals, one being exclusively homosexual with a biological base and the other being secondary homosexuals - not necessarily because of negative heterosexual experiences but possibly as a result of pleasant homosexual experiences. Quite frankly, we don't really know why people are homosexual at all. The popular stereotypes of butch lesbians and camp male homosexuals are not representative of homosexuals who include all personality types and people from all walks of life; homosexual dating agencies give perhaps the best evidence of this (Mullan 1984). As homosex-ual behaviour can be transient in adolescence and elective in single sex establishments, such as prisons, it is perhaps most useful for social workers to define homosexuality by the content of the individual's sexual imagery. In homosexuality, sexual fantasies are, of course, homosexual. Bisexual people are best explained, I think, simply as greedy people.

The problems of being homosexual

The single biggest problem about homosexuality is society's disapproval of it. The church openly condemns it, the law raises the age of consent from eighteen years to twenty-one years for male homosexuals, homophobia, ranging from "queer bashing" to ridicule, is common, and doctors and social workers will keep trying to cure people of homosexuality. Recently, a probation student dealing with a male homosexual convicted of "cottaging" was wildly enthusiastic about embarking upon lengthy psychotherapy with the man, delving into his family history. Quite sensibly, the chap moved to another town.

Society's inability to come to terms with the fact that homosexuality exists and is totally resistant to change makes it difficult for the homosexual to live an ordinary life. Social pressures tend to ensure that the fact of homosexuality becomes more than simply sexual choice and becomes the "whole person" rather than a part of the personality as is heterosexuality. It seems that homosexual men have more difficulty in coping with their sexual orientation and suffer more discrimination than do homosexual women. This is reflected in higher attempted suicide rates for homosexual men (Catalan 1983) and homosexual men are more likely to be homeless than homosexual women (Shanks 1982). Many homosexual men are pushed into marriage and they score highly on loneliness rates:

> .... they are more likely to cut themselves off more from
> any homosexual emotional attachments and possibly lack
> the ability to emotionally relate to their wives in terms of
> their total personality". (Ross 1983)

Health hazards, and public reaction to some illnesses, are different between the sexes. The incidence of sexually transmitted diseases, particularly syphilis, gonorrhoea and hepatitis B, has always been higher in homosexual men than in heterosexual men and women (Nichol Thin 1982). It is thought that there may be many factors to explain this, including the mode of sexual practice, multiple partners and anonymity of partners (Rompalo and Hunter Handsfield 1984). However, the promiscuity charge is a dangerous one as most studies have been carried out on city populations which only account for 5% of all male homosexuals (Llewellyn-Jones 1985).

There is no evidence that male homosexuals are unable to form long-term relationships but ageist attitudes amongst many male homosexuals, where youth and beauty is highly valued, may well be a factor in sexual behaviour (Plummer 1978). Also, people in a male, gay, city world may have little in common other than their homosexuality and their oppression. Being male and gay in a city may only offer casual contacts in gay pubs and clubs. Relationships embarked upon largely on the basis of physical attractiveness are likely to break down if there are no social or educational interests in common and in a climate which disapproves of such relationships.

Social disapproval of male homosexuals has increased to a point of hysteria with the recent spread of AIDS (acquired immune deficiency syndrome). This is a progressively debilitating condition which develops in a minority of people who are infected with a virus, HTLV-III/LAV (see Appendix 2.1 for details of mode of infection, antibody testing and management). Because it is a new and frightening disease, and probably also because innocent children have become infected via blood transfusions, homosexuals have found themselves being treated as virtual lepers. Sonnabend et al (1984) comment:

> *Suggesting that any particular group carries a specific*
> *infectious agent capable of causing severe immune*
> · *deficiency and cancer is a tremendously serious act.*
> *This is even more so if the group in question is already*
> *the object of discriminatory practice.*

And there is not sufficient evidence to hold male homosexuals solely responsible for the spread of AIDS. In fact, the recent media information about the spread of HTLV-111 has contributed to a drop in rates for other sexually transmitted diseases in male homosexuals (Weller et at 1984) and a recent study (Miller et al 1986) has shown that in identified seropositives - those with a positive antibody test result - high rates of safe sex behaviour change can be achieved if thorough counselling is provided after the results are given, with follow-up in peer group community organisations. Moral backlash campaigns do nothing to encourage male homosexuals to come forward for such helpful advice.

Unlike homosexual men, homosexual women rarely get sexually transmitted diseases such as syphilis, gonorrhoea, hepatitis, genital warts or herpes. They also suffer less from minor sexually transmitted diseases than do heterosexual women although they suffer a comparable incidence of psychiatric illness and an increased incidence of alcoholism (Degan and Waitkevitz 1982). This latter may be explained by their increased likelihood of visiting bars to meet women of the same sexual orientation. Most of the health vulnerability of homosexuals seems, therefore, to be at the door of the hazards of penile penetration and, most important, at the lack of permission to engage openly in a long-term, loving relationship with a person of the same sex. In this aspect, two women living together have an easier time of it than two men, although both are denied parenting opportunities.

There is no evidence to show that female homosexuals are any less satisfactory as parents than heterosexuals and their children are usually heterosexual (Green 1978, Golombok et al, in print) but, 'coming out of the closet" often means losing your children. Although as a general principle mothers are given custody and care and control of their children by the divorce courts, a recent survey (Lesbian Mothers on Trial 1984) revealed that forty-five percent of the lesbian mothers questioned lost care and control. Also, female homosexuals run risks when they try to become mothers. Using the services of the male homosexual community for "do-it-yourself" artificial insemination or picking up men for "one off" occasions raises health problems and the possibility of too small a gene pool (Hanscombe and Foster 1981). Few infertility clinics will accept female homosexuals for artificial insemination, although the BPAS is often helpful and sympathetic, and few social services departments will entertain the notion of homosexual fostering and adoptive parenting, although some London Boroughs have made tentative steps towards recruitment (Whitehouse 1985, Issues 1986).

What can social workers do?

Ideally, they shouldn't need to do anything at all but, in the current climate of opinion, there is a need for social workers to undertake a counselling and supportive role in coping with stigma and loss. Also many social workers are being pushed into supervisory roles in homosexual parenting situations. Plummer (1984) suggests that there are four reactions to the stigma of homosexuality; social workers should be aware of these because each brings special features which affect social work support efforts. He lists the reactions as denial, treatment, neutralisation and "coming to terms".

In denial, the homosexual is blocking the secret although there may be occasional "moral" holidays. This means that there are problems of isolation. This is particularly acute in instances of elderly homosexuals who may lose a partner but have no inheritance rights nor opportunity to grieve openly. Secret, homosexual grief needs recognising in depressed elderly people. Similarly, the married homosexual may need help. As Ross (1983) found, married homosexuals are more disturbed than unmarried homosexuals, although the strains of leading a conflicting existence are often taken care of by compartmentalism. Acknowledgement by social workers of the strains of denial can be helpful for homosexuals, although Plummer's next stage - treatment - is definitely unhelpful. Social work efforts to change homosexual orientation are a complete waste of time and homosexuals find them insulting (Fisher and Greenberg 1977; Raymond 1979); however, measures to assist with individual problems are helpful.

In the phase of neutralisation, Plummer is describing the process by which the homosexual behaviour is overt but the meaning is denied, e.g. "it happened but I was drunk". Here the social work task is a familiar one of supporting the client and helping them to face reality and stigmatising experiences. Good use can be made here of a variety of helping organisations such as CHE, Gemma, National Friend (see list of addresses in Appendix 2.2, at the end of the chapter), although social workers may hesitate to advise a young client in case he becomes at risk of conviction. For young people, there is a useful publication, Joint Council for Gay Teenagers, and most homosexuals in this phase would find Babuscio's book (1976) helpful.

It is at this time, too, that families are likely to need help. Parents Enquiry is a useful self-help organisation but parents need immediate and sensitive help to overcome their own feelings of grief and shock and retain their relationships with their children. Shernoff (1984) examines the impact on families of a parent or child "coming out" and suggests that family therapy techniques are appropriate in helping families cope with disclosure. Husbands and wives whose partner "comes out" have to face a strong feeling of rejection and lack of worth which needs attending to, regardless of how long the marriage had lasted and whether it was happy or not.

Plummer's final reaction, "coming to terms", allows the homosexual to recognise him/herself and is an important step in terms of self integrity. However, although isolation and denial are removed, it is hard to be homosexual "in public". As well as stigmatising experiences, there are a host of practical problems which range from the difficulties of obtaining a mortgage (difficult but not impossible for two women, possible for two men only if they can prove they do not have AIDS) to being a parent. A social work colleague who visited a female homosexual couple about the minor behavioural problems of their son (he probably would not have been referred if he had been living with a traditional couple) ended up giving long-term help and advice on artificial insemination, finance and sexual dysfunction. Having found him to be a credible worker in one area, the couple then shared their other problems with him. My colleague considers it all rather worthwhile; not only is it now a very happy family unit but it is a good model of how successful homosexual partnerships can be, given a little support and recognition.

Homosexuals of both sexes suffer from the same problems of sexual dysfunction as do heterosexuals. American homosexuals are increasingly accepted at sex therapy clinics following Masters and Johnson's lead (1970) but British homosexuals are much less likely to refer themselves to clinics, located as they are usually within the Family Planning Service. Social workers need, therefore, to be aware that their homosexual clients may need help and guidance in this area and be prepared to deal with such problems sympathetically and helpfully. Sexual dysfunction will be discussed more fully in Chapter 4.

Summary

The problems experienced by people with some degree of gender dysphoria, and their relatives, arise mainly from the illegitimacy of their sexual orientation and the stigma they suffer as a result of not conforming to accepted norms. Their dysphoria causes a "dysphoria" in our reactions - it unbalances us too, so we keep trying to make them "normal", to bring them back into line. This we cannot do at the current time because we do not know what causes transsexualism, transvestism nor homosexuality. All social workers can reasonably do is to exercise their skills in helping clients with the practical and emotional problems which arise from being "different" or being married to someone who is "different".

With adults whose degree of gender dysphoria is fairly obvious, the social work tasks are clear, albeit extraordinarily difficult; however, with confused, unhappy adolescents who cannot work out what their sexual orientation is, social workers need to tread with great care and ensure that the client's main problem is one of sexual confusion, not the result of an unhappy, disadvantaged and emotionally damaging home. On a positive note, social workers can recognise the importance of their becoming acquainted with the facts about health hazards and the possibility of them undertaking a serious role in health education.

References

Babuscio, J. (1976). *We Speak for Ourselves*. SPCK.

Bandura, A. & Walters, R. H. (1969). *Social Learning and Personality Development*. Holt, Rinehart & Winston.

Brierley, H. (1979). *Transvestism: a handbook with case studies for psychologists, psychiatrists and counsellors*. Pergamon.

Brierley, H. (1984). 'Gender Identity and Sexual Behaviour' in: *The Psychology of Sexual Diversity* (ed) Howell, K. Basil Blackwell.

Buhrich, N. (1986). 'Male-to-Female Transsexualism'. *British Journal of Sexual Medicine*. Feb, p52-54.

Catalan, J. (1983). 'Attempted Suicide and Homosexuality'. *British Journal of Sexual Medicine,* Feb, p11-14.

Chetwynd, J. & Harnett, O. (1978) (eds). *The Sex Role System*. Routledge & Kegan Paul.

Degan, K. & Waitkevitz (1982). 'Lesbian Health Issues'. *British Journal of Sexual Medicine*. May, p40-47.

Dewhurst, J. & Underhill, R. (1979). 'The suppression of facial hair growth in transsexuals using cyprotenone acetate'. *British Journal of Sexual Medicine*. Aug 1.

Erikson, E. (1948). *Children and Society*. Penguin.

Feldman, P. (1984). 'The Homosexual Response' in: *The Psychology of Sexual Diversity* (ed) Howell, K. Basil Blackwell.

Fisher, S. & Greenburg, R. P. (1977). *The Scientific Credibility of Freud's Theories and Therapies*. Harvest Press.

Goodman, R. (1982). 'How the GP Can Help Transsexuals'. *Pulse*. April 10, p77.

Golombok, S., Spencer, A. & Miller, M. (forthcoming). A comparison of 37 children of 27 lesbian mothers with 38 children of heterosexual mothers.

Green, R. (1978). 'Sexual Identity of 37 Children Raised by Homosexual or Transsexual Parents'. *American Journal of Psychiatry.* 135, 6, p692-7.

Green, R. (1981). 'Variant forms of human sexual behaviour' in: *Reproduction in mammals No 8 Human Sexuality* (eds) Austin, C. R. & Short, R. V. Cambridge University Press.

Hanscombe, G. E. & Foster, J. (1981). *Rocking the Cradle: Lesbian Mothers: A Challenge - Family Living.* Peter Owen.

Hoenig, J. & Kenna, J. C. (1974). "The prevalence of transsexualism in England and Wales'. *British Journal of Psychiatry,* 124, 181-190.

Issues (1986). *Social Services Insight,* 1(26) p3.

Joint Council for Gay Teenagers. *Breaking the Silence: Gay Teenagers Speak to Themselves.* BM JCGT, London WCIN 3XX.

Jones, E. (1927). "The early development of female sexuality'. *International Journal of Psychoanalysis,* 8, p459.

Kolodny, R., Masters, W. H. & Johnson, V. E. (1979). *Textbook of Sexual Medicine.* Little, Brown & Co.

Kline, P. (1972). *Fact and Fantansy in Freudian Theory.* Methuen.

Kohlberg, L. (1969). 'Stage and Sequence: the cognitive development approach to socialisation' in: *Handbook of Socialisation Theory and Research* (ed) Gostin, D. A. Rand McNally.

Lee, P. L. & Stewart, R. S. (1976) (eds). *Sex Differences: Cultural and Development Dimensions.* Urizen Books.

Lesbian Mothers on Trial (1984). *A Report on Lesbian Mothers and Child Custody.* Rights of Women, 52/54 Featherstone St., London EC1.

Llewellyn-Jones, D. (1985). *Herpes, AIDS and other sexually transmitted diseases.* Faber and Faber.

Lothstein, L. M. (1983). *Female-to-Male Transsexualism: Historical, Clinical and Theoretical Issues*. Routledge & Kegan Paul.

McFarlane, A. & Mugford, M. (1984). *British Counts: Statistics of Pregnancy and Childbirth*. HMSO.

Masters, W. H. & Johnson, V. (1970). *Human Sexual Inadequacy*. Little, Brown & Co.

Meyer, J. K. & Reter, D. J. (1979). 'Sex Reassignment'. *Archive of General Psychiatry*, 36, p1010-1915.

Miller, D., Green, J. & McCreaner, A. (1986). 'Organising a counselling service for AIDS & related problems'. *Genitourinary Medicine*. 62 114-119.

Money, J. (1973). 'Gender Role, Gender Identity, Core Gender Identity: Usage and Definition of Terms. *Journal of the American Academy of Psychoanalysis*, 1, p397-402.

Money, J. (1976). 'Two names, two wardrobes, two personalities'. *British Journal of Sexual Medicine*, 3,5, Oct.

Money, J. (1982). 'Introduction' in: *Men in Transition* (ed) Solomon, K. & Levy, B. Plenum Press.

Mullen, B. (1984). *The Mating Trade*. Routledge & Kegan Paul.

Nichol Thin, R. (1982). *Lecture Notes on Sexually Transmitted Disease*. Blackwell Scientific Publications.

Oakley, A. (1972). *Sex, Gender and Society*. Temple Smith.

Piaget, J. (1932). 'The Moral Judgement of the Child'. Macmillan.

Plummer, K. (1978). 'Men in Love' in: *The Couple* (ed) Corbin, M. Penguin.

Plummer, K. (1981) (ed). *The Making of the Modern Homosexual*. Hutchinson.

Prince, C. V. (1967). *The Transvestite and his Wife.* Argyle Books.

Randall, J. (1971). 'Indications for Sex Reassignment Surgery'. *Archive of Sexual Behaviour,* 1, 153-161.

Raymond, M. J. (1979). 'Sexual Fetishism'. *Update.* Dec, pp1205-1215.

Rompalo, A., & Hunter Handsfield, H. (1984). "Overview of Sexually Transmitted Diseases in Homosexual Men' in: *The Acquired Immune Deficiency Syndrome and Infections of Homosexual Men* (eds) Pearl, M. A. & Armstrong, D. Yorke Medical Books.

Ross, M. W. (1983). *The Married Homosexual Man.* RKP.

Shanks, N. J. (1982). 'Homosexuality amongst inmates of common lodging houses'. *British Journal of Sexual Medicine,* April, pp16-18.

Shernoff, M. J. (1984). 'Family Therapy for Lesbian and Gay Clients'. *Social Work.* July 29, 4, pp393-396.

Sonnabend, J. A., Witkin, S. S., & Purtilo, D. T. (1984). 'Acquired Immune Deficiency Syndrome (AIDS) - an explanation for its occurrence among homosexual men' in: *The Acquired Immune Deficiency Syndrome and Infections of Homosexual Men* (eds) Pearl, M. A. & Armstrong, D. Yorke Medical Books.

Stoller, R. J. (1978). 'The Gender Disorders' in *Sexual Deviation* (ed) Rosen, I. Oxford University Press, 2nd edition.

Tripp, C. A. (1977). *The Homosexual Matrix.* Quartet Books.

Weller, I. V. D., Hindley, D., Meldrum, J., & Adler, M. W. (1984). 'Gonorrhoea in homosexual men and media coverage of AIDS in London'. *British Medical Journal,* 289 1041.

Whitehouse, A. (1985). 'They said because we were gay they would not take the risk'. *Community Care.* May 30, pp20-22.

Williams, M. (1977). 'Psychological aspects of sexual medicine'. *British Journal of Sexual Medicine.* 4, 26, June.

Appendix 2.1

Acquired Immune Deficiency Syndrome (AIDS)

Attitudes

From a medical point of view, Aids is a new disease which has no established diagnostic hallmarks, eludes definition, has multiple diverse manifestations and is still developing (Sonnabend et al 1984). Its transmission requires very close personal contact so it is fairly easy to avoid becoming infected if sensible hygiene precedures are followed (DHSS 1985, DES 1986). From a public point of view, it is a new and frightening killer disease which seemed to affect promiscuous homosexuals but is now increasingly being transmitted to "innocent" people. Media coverage is lurid, exaggerated and often misinformative (CDSC 1985). Lack of confidence in government statements is such that the Sunday Mirror (June 29th 1986) actually stated:

> ...the horrifying extent of the disease and the ways
> it can be caught are being deliberately covered up
> by the worlds' governments.

Recent research into the attitudes of social work students about AIDS (Vass 1986) found that, although social workers are keen to offer help to victims and are critical of government and medical establishment initiatives, they too are terrified of contact with AIDS and misinformed on the subject. Seventy-two percent of the survey expressed very real worry about having to deal with a client who has AIDS. Thirty-two percent would be careful to keep their distance and seventeen percent would not even consider going near the person's home in case they caught the disease. Most would seek immediate medical attention if they even touched an AIDS sufferer and twenty-eight percent thought that the law should be used to control sufferers.

To some extent this is understandable. After all, none of us want to die a slow, painful and disfiguring death. But it is appalling that social workers too are subscribing to plague panic and regarding AIDS sufferers and virus carriers as virtual lepers. It is bad enough that the general public insist that earth on which contaminated blood has been spilt should be treated with a flame-thrower; it is distressing that parents remove their children from schools which contain haemophiliac pupils, but it is truly dreadful that social workers cannot bring themselves to offer help to sufferers. If everyone treats carriers as lepers, then carriers will become secretive about their condition, they will not receive counselling about sensible management and the actual risk of transmission will increase.

AIDS - What is it?

AIDS is a disease which leads to a lowering of the body's immunity to infection. It develops in a minority of people who are infected with Human-T-Lymphotropic Virus Type III or Lymphadenopathy Associated Virus (HTLV-III/LAV). The vast majority of people infected with HTLV-III/LAV (identified seropositives) either remain asymptomatic or suffer minor illnesses (DHSS 1985). The virus originated in Central Africa where it has a heterosexual spread but it became known as "the gay plague" because the earliest identified cases in the USA and Europe were homosexual men with multiple partners. In 1978, HTLV-III antibodies were detected in 1% of homosexual men attending a clinic for sexually transmitted diseases but the prevalence in 1984 was 65% (Donnelly et al 1985).

The virus is transmitted via infected body fluids, particularly blood and semen. Although the virus has been isolated in saliva and tears, there is no documented evidence of the spread of infection from these. Of all known cases of AIDS at February 1985, seventy-two percent in the USA and eighty-nine percent in the UK were either homosexual or bisexual. Haemophiliacs accounted for 1% in the USA and 2% in the UK. Intravenous drug users accounted for seventeen percent in the USA, with the rest being female partners of men at risk, children of infected partners, people with a central African or Haitian connection and a small minority of unknown cause (DHSS 1985). There is an antibody test for the HTLV-III/LAV virus, but not for AIDS. The results are difficult to interpret and of no use at all for those people who wish to use legal methods to restrain carriers. Although test results can be obtained within two weeks (Neville 1986), retesting is important because of the long incubation period and the number of false negative results. Even where the results are seropositive, this does not necessarily mean that the person currently harbours the virus or is infectious (Llewellyn-Jones 1985).

At Risk Groups

Because of the mode of infection, certain groups of people are at particular risk. These are:

Homosexuals and their Partners

HTLV-III/LAV can be transmitted via semen, so people who indulge in anal intercourse are particularly at risk. The anal mucosa is much more likely to be damaged than the vaginal mucosa (Nichol Thin 1982), so the risk to female partners of infected men is lower than that to male partners. Also, receptive anal intercourse is a high risk factor whilst insertive anal intercourse is is not a risk factor (DHSS 1985). As mentioned earlier, sensitive counselling and the encouragement of safe sex behaviour (particularly the use of a condom) reduces the incidence of all sexually transmitted diseases in homosexual males.

Blood Transfusion Recipients

No blood transfusion recipients in the UK have contacted AIDS, although haemophiliacs have been infected in some cases. The risk from this source has now been removed by the screening of all blood donations for the virus antibody. There is the possibility of accidental transmission of the virus to people with skin wounds in their handling of AIDS sufferers or identified seropositives. This is extremely slight, with only one documented case in the USA. In one hospital in the USA dealing with AIDS patients, eighty-five nursing staff suffered thirty-three accidental needle stick injuries, but none of them became seropositive over three years (Hirsch et al 1985).

Drug Misusers

The virus can be transmitted via the sharing of contaminated needles and syringes amongst drug misusers. This category of people accounted for seventeen percent of all known AIDS cases in the USA at February 1985 (DHSS 1985) and is becoming the greatest at risk group in this country. Over seventy percent of drug misusers in Edinbirgh are estimated to be seropositive (Blyth and Milner 1986) and it is this category of people who face the greatest risk of accidental transmission. Female drug misusers who turn to prostitution to support their habit are a potential threat, but even more worrying for social workers is the likelihood of the transmission of the virus from an infected mother to her infants during pregnancy or birth or possibly through breast milk. The heroin addict mother who is challenging the social services care order on her infant in the higher Courts already poses a difficult legal and ethical dilemma. How much more worrying will decision-making be about an infant born to a mother who is both a drug addict and an HTLV-III/LAV carrier? And what future could the infant look forward to if societal attitudes are not modified? Is such a child to be debarred from schooling altogether?

Artificial Insemination Recipients

Four Australian recipients of frozen semen from a symptomless carrier of HTLV-III have developed antibodies to the virus (Stewart et al 1985) and the DHSS has now issued guidelines for doctors involved in artificial insemination (DHSS 1986). They recommend antibody testing of all donors, with repeat tests after three months, before frozen semen can be used. Where fresh semen is used, they recommend that donors are advised of the possible risks. There is no guarantee of total safety. It is difficult to predict whether these procedures will reduce the number of volunteer donors or the number of couples eager for artificial insemination. However, whatever happens, there is likely to be an effect on social workers. Either there will be an increase in the numbers of worried parents or an increase in the numbers of couples applying for fostering and adoption.

Not At Risk Groups

There have been no known cases of infection in casual person-to-person contact in schools nor in the intimate contact of a family setting containing an infected member. The virus is not transmitted via normal social contact, airborne droplets from coughing and sneezing, sharing washing or toilet facilities, sharing eating and dining utensils, or living in the same house. Accidental transmission is extremely rare but it would seem sensible to discourage young people from having tatoos, ear piercing or sharing razors and toothbrushes. Social workers dealing with disturbed or alienated youngsters vulnerable to casual sexual contact or drug misuse should certainly be undertaking health education aimed at minimising risks of infection.

Management

Not only is AIDS extremely difficult to catch, it is extremely easy to deal with AIDS sufferers or HTLV-III/LAV carriers without shunning them. Should residential workers with a seropositive haemophiliac have to deal with spilt contaminated body fluids, then they simply need a bottle of bleach and some disposable cloths. If the worker has a cut or abrasion, then he or she should keep this covered while handling the infected person. The most difficult group to deal with will be children with behaviour problems, such as spitting and scratching, but here again it seems that sensible hygienic precautions will be sufficient. Details of these are outlined in the two excellent Health Education booklets which are available from:

DHSS Store, Health Publications Unit, No 2 Site,
Manchester Road, Heywood, Lancs OL10 1PZ.
Quote reference CMO (86) 10 for
Children at school and problems related to AIDS
and CMO (85) 7 for *Aids Booklet 1.*

Counselling

There is a great need for social workers to become involved in the counselling of HTLV-III/LAV carriers. Such people need help with their fear of dying and of society's reactions. They also need to be encouraged to tell their dentists, be careful in affectionate contact, be scrupulous about hygiene and first aid, and consider carefully their sexual behaviour. The problems involved in being a carrier are not insuperable but the stigma is such that very sensitive help is essential.

Social workers also need to think out very carefully their own attitudes. As mentioned earlier, the antibody test does not give a clear indication of what is to happen and social workers should resist strongly public demands to have this information available on every vulnerable child and adult. For those social workers unable to cope with the problem, community group counselling and information are available from:

Terrence Higgins Trust Ltd, DM AIDS, 34 South Moulton Street, London WC1N 3X.

Haemophilia Society, PO Box 9, 16 Trinity Street, London SE1 1DE.

References

Blyth, E. & Milner, J. (forthcoming) 'Poor Little Bleeders'. *Times Educational Supplement.*

Communicable Disease Surveillance Centre (1985) *The Acquired Immune Deficiency Syndrome.* February.

DES (1986) *Children at school and problems related to AIDS.*

DHSS (1985) *Acquired Immune Deficiency Syndrome (AIDS); General Information for Doctors.* May.

DHSS (1986) *Acquired Immune Deficiency Syndrome (AIDS) Booklet 4;* Guidance for Doctors and A.I. Clinics. July.

Donnelly, P., Irving, W., & Starke, I. (1985) *Infection and the Immunocompromised Patient.* Current Medical Literature Ltd.

Hirsch, M.S., Wormser, G.P., Schooley, R.T. et al (1985) 'Risk of nosocomial infection with human T-cell lymphotropic virus III'. *New England Journal of Medicine,* 312, pp1-4.

Llewellyn-Jones, D. (1985) *Herpes, AIDS and other sexually transmitted diseases.* Faber and Faber.

Neville, R.G. (1986) 'The Aids Problem - What the GP can do?'. *The Physician,* 5(7), pp895-897

Nichol Thin, R. (1982) *Lecture Notes on Sexually Transmitted Diseases.* Basil Blackwell Scientific Publications.

Sonnabend, J.A., Witkin, S.S. & Purtilo, D.T. (1984) 'Acquired Immune Deficiency Syndrome (AIDS) - an explanation for its occurrence among homosexual men' in *The Acquired Immune Deficiency Syndrome and Infections of Homosexual Men.* Eds Pearl, M.A. & Armstrong, D. Yorke Medical Books.

Stewart, G.J., Tyler, J.P.P., Cunningham, A.L. et al, 'Transmission of human T-cell lymphotropic virus type III (HTLV III) by artificial insemination by donor'. *Lancet* ii, pp581-585.

Vass, A.A. (1986) *Aids: A Plague in us; A Social Perspective.* Venus Academica

Appendix 2.2

Useful Addresses

1. Rape Crisis Centre, PO Box 69, London WC1X 9NS
   Tel: Office: 01 278 3956, 24 hrs: 01 837 1600

2. Incest Survivors Campaign, c/o 48 William IV Street,
   London WC1

3. The Beaumont Society, BM Box Hasar, London WC1.

4. SHAFT (The Self-Help Association for Transsexuals),
   4 Adelaide Square, Windsor, Berks SL4 2AQ.
   Tel: Windsor 67263

5. Parent Enquiry (for parents of homosexuals): Rose Robertson,
   16 Hornley Road, Catford, London SE6 2HZ

6. Campaign for Homosexual Equality (CHE), 33 King Street,
   Manchester M60 2EL, Tel: 061 228 1985 and
   22 Great Windmill Street, London W1, Tel 01 402 6750

7. Gemma (disabled and ablebodied lesbians), BM Box 5700,
   London WC1N 3XX

8. Gay Icebreakers, BM Gay Lib, London WX1N 3XX, 01 274 9590

9. Action for Lesbian Parents, c/o Women's Centre, Moor Lane,
   Lancaster

10. Advisory Service for Gay People with a drinking problem,
    041 770 6599

11. AA Manchester Gay Group, Church Army Hostel,
    Plymouth Grave, 061 273 4360

12. The August Trust, Secretary, 20 Orchard Rise East, Black Fen,
    North Sidcup, Kent, 01 736 6602

13. Friend, 274 Upper Street, London N1, 01 359 7371/2

14. Gaydaid (help for gay disabled people), Write (SAE) c/o Trevor, 34 Pembroke Street, Bedford, MK40 3RH, 0234 58879

15. Gay Bereavement Support Group, Unitarian Rooms, Hoop Lane, London NW11 8BD, 01 837 7324

16. Gay Doctors in England, c/o Martin Farrell, 13 Radcliffe Court, Rose Crescent, Cambridge, CB2 3LR

17. GLAD (gay legal advice), BM Glad, London WC1N 3XX, 01 821 7672

18. Irish Gay Switchboard (IGRM), PO Box 739, Dublin 8, 01 786593

19. Lesbian Line, BM Box 1514, London WC1N 3XX, 01 837 8602

20. Married Gays, c/o London Friend, 274 Upper Street, London N1. 01 359 7371

21. SIGMA (support for heterosexuals in mixed relationships), BM Sigma, London WC1N 3XX, 01 837 7324

Chapter Three

Non-Violent Sex Crimes

This chapter covers the third area of my classification, namely variant sexual behaviour which affects men only and which may be open to some change.

Social workers not infrequently have clients who seems to be mild, ineffectual men who cannot be compared in any way with the highly aggressive and exploitive sex offenders outlined in Chapter One but whose sexually variant behaviour means that they constitute a menace to society: the so-called average sex offender - the exhibitionist, peeping tom, paedophile, etc. Whilst this behaviour can, and often is, explained as the means by which a sexually low-powered or frightened man can gain sexual satisfaction without needing to make personal, intimate contact with women, nevertheless the expression of this sexual behaviour often frightens other people. A man making an obscene phone call may well be terrified of women and present as woefully inadequate to his social worker, but the person on the receiving end of the phone call will have been disturbed and probably frightened. Therefore, social workers are expected to "do something" about such clients.

What they actually "do" is often not very effective and certainly not very scientific because we undertand so little about such behaviour, except that it is relatively common but only in males. Whilst one could argue that women have opportunities for exhibitionism in everyday life - from low cut dresses to stripping - and therefore the behaviour is not sex specific, this argument simply doesn't hold up. The behaviour is always male and heterosexual, albeit of a rather stunted type. Inadequate male homosexuals do not go around exhibiting themselves to men or peeping through their bedroom curtains. The fact that it is peculiarly male behaviour and fairly common contributes to it being ignored at many levels. Whilst the percentage of men whose behaviour actually offends against the law and who are caught is relatively small, most men seem to indulge in some form of masturbatory fantasy which has little direct link with heterosexual intercourse and "biological" sexual cues - as a persusal of porno-graphic magazines shows. This ranges from a simple but common fetish about high heels to extremely bizarre, autoerotic behaviour which is only revealed when the activity leads to accidental deaths - through self-strangulation, for example.

Neither do men find this sort of behaviour at all difficult to believe. Unlike serious sexual assault, there is rarely any burden of proof on the victim before prosecution is considered. In fact, one subject quoted by Luria and Rose (1979) suggests that a raped woman should accuse the rapist of "flashing" as she would then save herself much agony and the offender would be dealt with immediately. Men accept that they have a capacity for a wide and varied range of sexual behaviour and male theorists acknowledge this. Kinsey (1948), for example, argues that it is not difficult to explain why the human animal does a particular thing sexually but that it is consider-ably more difficult to explain why each and every individual is not involved in every type of sexual activity. Similarly, Beach (1977) says that we should make an important distinction between appetitive behaviour and consumatory behaviour, the latter being the same for everyone, i.e. orgasm, but the appetitive behaviour being subject to very wide variations. They both forget that what they are actually talking about is mankind, not humankind. Perhaps they should study women's sexual behaviour and find out why women do not develop fetishes nor indulge in peeping.

Men seem very dismissive about this whole area of behaviour. One major text (Freedman 1983) deals with "other sexual variations" in a single paragraph:

> The offenders are generally inadequate individuals with marked feelings of inferiority, and are unable to express themselves sexually except by masturbatory activities in association with their deviant behaviour.

Are we then supposed to ignore them just because they are understandable but inferior as men? Certainly the experts are losing interest in them, although this process may well have been hastened by their resistiveness to traditional psychiatric treatment. The trend seems to be to redefine their behaviour. Instead of referring to perversions or aberrations, the term "paraphilia" now seems the most accepted one (derived from Greek words meaning "alongside of" and "love") and Kolodny (1979) suggests that this relatively neutral word serves to minimise difficulties in treatment.

Even standard psychiatric texts are accepting a redefinition of the behaviour. Bebbington and Hill (1985) refer to this behaviour simply as socially unacceptable behaviour which should only be treated if the patient is well motivated. They also say that the aims for psychiatrists in this area are "to make the deviation and its implications more tolerable for the patient". This emphasis on better adjustments avoids all the ethical and scientific issues involved in trying to change individuals; it ignores especially the effects on women who are left with no alternative but to have unlisted telephone numbers and draw their bedroom curtains tightly. It also writes off a whole group of men as inferior and unworthy.

Difficult though work in this area is, there are a few alternatives to either suppressing the behaviour or aiming for better adjustment; these will be discussed below in terms of what is known about the effective treatment of male sex offenders whose behaviour involves distancing themselves from women. The behaviour seems to fall into two main groups - one in which women are substituted by other objects, that is fetishism, including transvestism and paedophilia; and that which is basically hostile, such as exhibitionism and frotteurism. The first is the most difficult to quantify, explain and change.

Fetishism

Raymond (1979) defines fetishism as "the propensity to be sexually stimulated by some special part or peculiarity of the body, or by some inanimate object". This definition could cover a lot of sexual behaviour but a fetish is only really a fetish when the stimulus is not a clear sex signal and it is not a person as a whole who is being responded to. So, being a "legs" or "bottom man" does not mean that one is a fetishist, but stealing knickers from clothes lines and taking them home to stroke is definitely fetishism, and probably the most common fetishist a social worker will deal with professionally. People with foot fetishes, particularly those where the person has a desire to remove shoes from the feet of a complete stranger, also get referred to social workers, but my experience of foot fetishes has been limited to children - of both sexes and brain damaged.

Standard texts on fetishism usually include a wide range of behaviours; for example, Gosselin and Wilson (1980) include sadomasochism in this category because the behaviour is mainly concerned with sexual fantasy and, despite lurid media messages, rarely involves any real pain. Fetishes most commonly include speciality garments (mainly leather, rubber or vinyl), stolen underwear, specific fabrics (where all the clothing is of one fabric), belittling costumes and bondage. Spengler's study (1977) found that whips, canes and bonds were the most popular items but they were used symbolically in the main; but I would have reservations about including sadomasochism in the "fetish" category as it involves both heterosexual and homosexual males.

Gosselin and Wilson (1984) regard fetishistic behaviour as implicating some sort of imprinting, although they have no real evidence for this view, and psychoanalytic theory explains it as a cover for repressed homosexual and sadistic drives. McGuire et al (1965) propose a straightforward learning theory explanation, i.e. the young child comes into contact with a random stimulus that causes the first significant sexual arousal. This single pairing of situation and arousal is insufficient to lead to variant behaviour but the memory of the erotic event becomes part of a later masturbatory fantasy. Repeated masturbation in which this fantasy becomes prominent could gradually give enormous erotic power to the variant stimulus and other reinforcements could crystallise the variant fantasy, such as initial failure at heterosexual intercourse. They argue that the behaviour is male specific because boys masturbate earlier, more easily and more frequently than girls (who also often masturbate without fantasy, recorded by Kinsey 1953 and Hite 1976) and boys have more pressure on them to succeed.

They recommend treatment by covert sensitisation in which the subject imagines an aversive scene immediately after being presented with a sexually arousing scene, either visually or by fantasy, and aversion relief therapy. This explanation and therapy gains some support from Raymond (1979) who found that fetishists responded well to aversion therapy with good long-term results. He also found that the treatment of fetishism in this way did not release homosexual or sadistic drives although, of course, removing an undesirable behaviour pattern does not automatically establish a new, desirable one.

Many theorists regard transvestism as a fetish and this is supported by Gosselin and Wilson's surprise finding (1980) that fetishistic behaviour can produce relaxation as well as arousal. Certainly transvestism seems to start out in this way although the erotic content of cross-dressing seems to disappear as the transvestism progresses (Brierley 1979, 1984). Whilst acknowledging the fetishistic elements of the behaviour, it does not seem appropriate for social workers to attempt aversion therapy with transvestites, especially as the fetishistic behaviour is likely to cease anyway. As suggested in Chapter Two, the main role for the social worker is a counselling one.

Odd though it may seem to discuss transvestism under more than one heading, the classification of paedophilia as a fetish must seem even odder. It is certainly a view which the Paedophile Information Exchange members would hotly dispute. Some writers on the subject would argue that I am taking for granted a consensus view of the role of the child in the family in modern society and that a conflict model would challenge various structural factors in relation to the power of the family (Hart 1981) or even see the family as obsolete (Gough & MacNair, 1984) leading to a redefinition of childhood and children's needs. Many paedophiles believe that children not only have sexual needs but that they would benefit from loving, sexual relationships with adults (O'Carroll 1980). And they have convinced a major researcher in the field that the notion of boys needing the companionship, example and sexual tutoring of older males in order to learn the "tribal" rules has some validity (Rossman 1984). Until recently, many paedophiles actively campaigned for the social accept- ance of paedophilia, a ridiculously optimistic view which seems to support the more traditional view that paedophiles do not cope well with adult relationships.

Paedophilia here does not include homosexuality nor the sexual abuse of children described earlier. I am referring to people who are heterosexual but who fail in adult relationships and who are attracted to children because they lack adult characteristics and are non- threatening. The sexual behaviour most commonly involves stroking, as in other fetishistic behaviour. The child, like the inanimate object of the "ordinary" fetishist, replaces the usual sexual object. The peak of interest is reached for the paedophile in 10-11 year old girls and 12 year old boys (PIE, 1975) and the reason why many paedophiles prefer boys is not necessarily a homosexual orientation at all but because paedophilies, who cannot cope with adult women, may well feel that they understand boys better than girls. And the myth of the dirty old man in easily dimissed; most paedophiles commit their offences before forty years of age although only about five percent occur before adolescence (Burgess et al 1978). This survey identifies three types of paedophile:

fixated | originating in childhood, largely inadequate individuals who are overwhelmed by the ordinary demands of life;

regressed | often a married man who is depressed at the time of the offence, which takes place during a situational crisis. The usual reaction is deep shame and disgust. Burgess et al suggest that this group responds best to therapeutic efforts because they are able to acknowledge their part in the event; and

exploitative | involving force and violence. An unusual and atypical paedophile who would be better categorised under the coercive offenders category.

One of the main problems in dealing with paedophilia is that paedophiles see their victims as seductive or, at best, less than innocent (Rossman 1984). This is not borne out by studies of victims. Whilst victims usually know the paedophile socially, most commonly via church, youth clubs or relatives, they tend to be either emotionally deprived or unsupervised children. Howells (1979) found that in both instances the children accepted the sexual advances because they were looking for affectionate not sexual relationships. After an assault, the child tends to suffer from all the fuss involved, constant retelling of the incident and the trauma of a court appearance. Ingram (1979) found these aspects to be more damaging to the children than the actual assault which was usually fairly slight. The main role for social workers must be the careful organisation of the subsequent handling of the child and several of the "how to say no" books currently on sale tackle many of the issues of what to do about too friendly helpers on camping holidays and intrusive baby sitters.

Paedophiles are probably the least aggressive of all child molesters but they suffer most from public hostility. They are at the bottom of prison pecking orders and they suffer from physical assault, isolation, secrecy and, sometimes, shame (Plummer 1981). However, children can be protected (a consumer guide to the use of "say no" books and videos is given in Appendix 3.1 at the end of this chapter) and paedophiles do respond to therapy, particularly if they can accept that their behaviour is extremely socially unacceptable and not necessarily compulsive. Although neither psychotherapy nor aversion therapy (often very little different from punishment in this context) have been found to be very effective, social workers are finding social skills training a useful therapy. An experiment undertaken at Broadmoor (Crawford & Allen 1979) which focused on direct instruction, modelling role playing, feedback and reinforcement, together with a general widening of the prisoners' social horizons, showed good results. The Lancaster IT Model (Denham) should be equally appropriate for use with paedophiles, who also seem to benefit from training in non-verbal and verbal skills in relation to communication with women and from behaviour therapy aimed at counter-conditioning masturbatory fantasies.

Exhibitionism, Voyeurism and Frotteurism

These behaviours all involve the maintenance of distance from women in sexual encounters and they create two problems, firstly for the offender who is not coping with his adult sexuality, and secondly for the women unwillingly involved in a hostile act. Exhibitionists seem to be the largest group but this may be because they are the most likely to be detected. Exhibitionism most commonly takes the form of "flashing" although occasionally it takes the form of defaecating in front of women. Although aggressive, it is slightly different from "doing a mooney" which does not seem to have direct sexual connotations nor stimulation. Exhibitionism is most common in adolescence and is usually outgrown with only twenty percent of all offenders becoming persistent (Burgess et al 1978). Voyeurism (peeping) and frotteurism (rubbing up against women in crowded places) are less easily detected, although they are, like obscene phone calls, very distressing to women.

Psychotherapy and psychodrama seem to have little effect on these behaviours although some behaviour therapists, particularly those using aversion therapy and counter education, have claimed some success (Reswick & Wolfgang 1972). The most successful form of behaviour therapy seems to be that which focuses on the covert behaviour (McGuire et al 1965), because the masturbatory fantasies seem to maintain the habit strength of the deviant behaviour (Evans 1970). Drugs have proved moderately successful in the treatment of voyeurism and exhibitionism, but Cooper (1978) recommends that they should not be prescribed for more than six months in view of their dangerous effects. They may lower the sex drive but there is the risk of breast enlargement, testicular atrophy and bone degeneration (Gunn 1980), side-effects which would only produce a further set of problems for both the client and social worker. Social skills work has yet to be seriously tried on this group of offenders, although it would seem a logical method, especially as one long running group for non-violent sex offenders which focuses on sharing, broadening social activities and personal support has had some success in reducing recidivism and removing the offenders' belief in the compulsive nature of the behaviour (Weaver & Fox 1984). They have discovered, however, that the work needs to be long-term with a high degree of commitment from the workers as well as the clients.

Although these behaviours are open to some change, good results are few and far between. Bancroft (1974) comments:

> ... it is clear not only that progress in understanding has
> been minimal and is likely to be slow in the future but also
> we have achieved little in the way of useful outcome research.
> On the credit side, we now have a variety of techniques each
> of which has been found to be useful in certain cases.

Social workers undertaking work in this area need to be aware of their own values and the high degree of commitment required for both the client and the therapist. For those who wish to undertake such work, Bancroft (1974) suggests that the process is easier if the social worker helps the client to define his goals and if two principles are observed, firstly in aiming to improve heterosexual relationships rather than first reducing deviant behaviour, and secondly in setting quite limited, progressive goals. He cautions against trying to work with clients over thirty-five years of age, who would require a whole life change, and with those who are depressed.

Summary

I hope that the fact that this is a short chapter does not signify that I too seem to dismiss this group of offenders as simply male inadequates. Rather, it reflects the lack of knowledge about, interest in, and commitment to the treatment of such offenders. I protest about a whole group of men being written off because their behaviour embarrasses men and by whose standards they fall woefully short. I hope that social workers will contribute towards the literature and will try to effect improvements in this area.

However, I do feel that any great improvement and knowledge will not necessarily come from studying sex offenders of this type in an individual, pathological way. We really should be addressing the question of why women don't commit sex offences of this nature and asking ourselves how men can be more easily successful in the male role. At the moment it is rather like most male-directed research; it presupposes some sort of acceptable, white, male, heterosexual norm. I am greatly cheered by the research of a black female colleague of mine; she is researching why black people succeed. I would hope that future research identifies what men need to do to succeed as men rather than continue to concentrate on their manifest failures.

References

Bancroft, J. (1974). *Deviant Sexual Behaviour: Modification and Assessment.* Clarendon Press.

Beach, F. A. (1977). *Human Sexuality in Four Perspectives.* John Hopkins Press.

Bebbington, P. E. & Hill, P. D. (1985). *A Manual of Practical Psychiatry.* Blackwell Scientific Publications.

Brierley, H. (1979). *Transvestism: a handbook with case studies for psychologists, psychiatrists and counsellors.* Pergamon.

Brierley, H. (1984). 'Gender Identity and Sexual Behaviour' in: *The Psychology of Sexual Diversity* (ed) Howell, K. Basil Blackwell.

Burgess, A. N., Groth, A. N. Holmstrom, L. L. & Sgroi, S. M. (1978). *Sexual Assault of Children and Adolescents.* Lexington.

Cooper, A. (1978). 'Anti-androgens in general practice'. *British Journal of Sexual Medicine,* 42, 5 Nov.

Crawford, D. & Allen, J. (1979). 'A Social Skills Training Programme with Sex Offenders' in: *Love and Attraction* (eds) Cook, M. & Wilson, G. Pergamon

Denham, G. *Intensive Intermediate Treatment with Juvenile Offenders: a handbook on assessment and group work practice.* Centre of Youth, Crime and Community, University of Lancaster.

Evans, D. R. (1970). 'Subject Variables and Treatment Effects in Aversion Therapy'. *Behavioural Research & Therapy,* 8, pp147-52.

Freedman, G. R. (1983). *Sexual Medicine.* Churchill Livingstone.

Gosselin, C. & Wilson, G. (1980). *Sexual Variations.* Faber & Faber.

Gosselin, C. & Wilson, G. (1984). 'Fetishism and Sadomasochism' in: *The Psychology of Sexual Diversity* (ed) Howell, K. Basil Blackwell.

Gough, J. & McNair, M. (1984). *Gay Liberation in the Eighties.*
Pluto Press.

Gunn, J. (1980). *Sexual Offenders.* Mims Magazine, 1 Dec, p47-53.

Hart, J. (1981). 'Social Workers and Paedophiles: Some Dilemmas',
in: *Perspectives on Paedophilia* (ed) Taylor, B. Batsford Academic.

Hite, S. (1976). *The Hite Report.* Macmillan.

Howells, K. (1979). 'Some meanings of children for paedophiles' in:
Love and Attraction (ed) Cook, M. & Wilson, G. Pergamon.

Ingram, M. (1979). 'Sociological Aspects: the participatory victim'.
British Journal of Sexual Medicine, 44, 6 Jan.

Kinsey, A. C., Pomeroy, W. B. & Martin, C. E. (1948).
Sexual Behaviour in the Human Male. W. B. Saunders & Co.

Kinsey, A. C., Pomeroy, W. B., Martin, C. E. & Gebhard, P. H. (1953).
Sexual Behaviour in the Human Female. W. B. Saunders & Co.

Kolodny, R., Masters, W. H. & Johnson, V. E. (1979). *Textbook of
Sexual Medicine.* Little, Brown Co.

Luria, Z. & Rose, M. D. (1979). *Psychology of Human Sexuality.*
Wiley.

McGuire, R. J., Carlisle, J. M. & Young, B. G. (1965). 'Sexual
deviation as conditioned behaviour: a hypothesis'. *Behavioural
Research & Therapy,* 2, pp185-190.

O'Carroll, T. (1980). *Paedophilia - The Radical Case.* Peter Owen.

Paedophile Information Exchange (1975). *Survey of Members*

Plummer, K. (1981). 'The Paedophiles Progress: the view from
below' in: *Perspective on Paedophilia* (ed) Taylor, B.
Batsford Acadamic.

Raymond, M. J. (1979). 'Sexual Fetishism'. *Update,* 1 Dec,
pp1205-1215.

Reswick, H. L. S. & Wolfgang, M. E. (1972). *Treatment of Sex Offenders.* Little, Brown Co.

Rossman, P. (1984). *Sexual Experience Between Men and Boys.* Temple Smith.

Spengler, A. (1977). ' Manifest Sadomasochism in Males: results of an empirical study '. *Archive of Sexual Behaviour,* 6, pp441-56.

Weaver, C., & Fox, C. (1984). 'The Berkeley Sex Offenders Group: a seven year evaluation'. *Probation Journal.* Vol 31, No4, pp143-146.

Appendix 3.1

"Consumer Guide"

The recognition of the scale of sexual abuse of children has given rise to a very real concern that something practical should be done to protect children in an active and positive way. The expression of this concern has led to the proliferation of "say no" booklets, videos, story and colouring books, drama workshops, and anatomically correct dolls. For the social worker who may be bewildered by the sheer volume and diversity of the material and who is unsure how to select and use it appropriately, I offer this brief "consumer guide" based on the practical experience of students and social workers in the Huddersfield area over the last year.

Prevention

The literature seems to indicate that prevention is most effective at the peak ages for onset of abuse, i.e. when the child is three to five years old and nine to eleven years old (Koblinsky & Behana, 1984). With the younger age group, the topic is best discussed in the same manner as any small child safety topic, along the lines of what to do if you get lost, what to do if you see a fire, etc. Two activity books are readily available in supermarkets and bookshops in this country:

> It's OK to Say No! Peter Haddock Ltd
> Colouring Book and Activity Book, both priced approx. 70p

The books are identical in story content and illustrations and give realistic information. However, workers have found the colouring book, aimed at young children, the better of the two. The activity book seems to be aimed at school age children and general experience shows that the activities break up the sequence of "say no" statements with the result that the "message" is lost. Some of the activities are quite difficult, particularly the word searches, and some are rather silly; for example, the message at the top of one page is "But another kind of touching can be scary" and the activity at the bottom of the page is "Join the dots and find where the man is".

The best book I have seen for small children, and tested on "ordinary" children, is a Canadian one, Freeman, L. (1982) *Its My Body,* Parenting Press Inc, a delightfully presented book similar in style to any information book for this age range. It is accompanied by an explanatory booklet, Hart-Rossi, J. (1984) *Protecting Your Child From Sexual Abuse,* Parenting Press.

Older children are able to cope with a more direct approach and the story book, Watcher, O. (1983) *No More Secrets for Me,* Viking Kestrel, which contain a selection of stories for children of different ages and in different situations, has been found useful. However, social workers complain about the cost (over £9) and that it is rather middle class. Children of this age also respond positively to the Rolf Harris Video: *Kids Can Say No,* available from Rolf Harris Video, 43 Drury Lane, London WC2B 5RT. It should be used in conjunction with follow-up discussion and there is an accompanying booklet, Porter, R. (ed) (1984) *Child Sexual Abuse Within the Family,* Tavistock. This is a useful overview but workers need to use it with caution as it seems to support a mother-blaming attitude. Both the story book and video should ideally be used as part of general sex education with this age group.

Detection and Intervention

For an excellent outline on techniques for opening up discussion in this difficult area, there is Michelle Elliott's *Preventing Child Sexual Assault, a practical guide to talking with children,* Bedford Square Press NCVO. This is very good value at only £2.50 from bookshops or £2.80 by post from MacDonald & Evans Distribution Services Ltd, Estover Road, Plymouth PL6 7PZ. Michelle Elliott also runs the Kidscape Campaign which educates adults and children by means of drama workshops.

For individual children who need to be able to talk about their experiences not only for detection purposes but also for therapeutic reasons - they usually feel guilty - the use of anatomically correct dolls, of appropriate ethnic origin, is extremely effective. As there are dangers in using these dolls, inexperienced workers would be advised to consult with their local NSPCC service for guidance. In Leeds, the NSPCC have also found that adults benefit from using the dolls and from play therapy generally as it allows mothers to express their impotence and anger and helps father to appreciate the physical size difference between them and the children they have abused. For workers who have no easy access to NSPCC expertise, there are two excellent articles, Bannister, A. (1985) Monster Man Has Gone, *Community Care,* 28th Nov, and Baker, A. (1986) The Power of Play, *Community Care,* 23rd Jan, which are discussed in Chapter One.

Reference

Koblinsky, S. & Behana, N. (1984). 'Child Sexual Abuse: the educator's role in prevention, detection and intervention'. *Young Children.* September.

Chapter Four

Sexual Dysfunction

So far, I have concentrated on people whose behaviour has been generally considered to be outside the norm of expected and accepted sexual behaviour. In this chapter, I wish to concentrate on "normal" couples who are experiencing problems in engaging in sexual intercourse to their own satisfaction. I wish to discuss whether this is really a problem or whether it is largely manufactured by media messages and whether it is a problem in which social workers should be involved at all. The ideal norms for couples seems to consist of a notion that one man and one woman will become physically and emotionally attracted to one another, that they will engage largely in monogamous activity, in private, over a long period of time. This activity is commonly thought to follow a steady curve from initial, blissful excitement, gradually tapering down to a state of lowered activity but steady affection. If hiccups occur in this process, we tend to explain them away in terms of men desiring more sexual encounters than women or view them as problems of individual pathology. Yet the reality is that sexual hiccups occur on a massive scale and most people suffer in silence.

The evidence for this was forced upon us initially by a series of American surveys about sexual behaviour. The first of these (Kinsey et al, 1948, 1953) not only shocked people with details of a high incidence of "rare" behaviours such as homosexuality, child abuse, masturbation, etc., but they also revealed that factors such as religious orthodoxy and devotion could seriously inhibit successful sexual behaviour in adult life. As this finding did not accord with our happy myths about loving couples, married in church and living happily ever after, those people who complained about their unhappy sex lives were considered rather unusual for many years and, for the most part, tended to receive therapy of a psychoanalytic kind. This therapy did not prove to be very effective in the treatment of sexual dysfunction. As Luria and Rose (1979) point out:

After six or seven years, a patient might feel that his premature ejaculation came from confusing and contradictory sexual fantasies of causing pain and disappointment to a woman, probably his mother. He might even feel comfortable about his insights. But he may continue to ejaculate prematurely nonetheless.

Psychoanalysis is neither appropriate nor efficient for dealing with problems which are extremely common. And dissatisfaction with one's sex life is the most common marital problem (Stuart and Hammond 1980), although it does not necessarily stem from personal inadequacy or marital discord. Although one third of all marriages break down (OPCS 1983), sexual difficulty is not the main cause. It has been estimated that every other couple struggle with a sexual problem at some time in their relationship (Masters & Johnson 1966; Frank, Anderson & Kupfer 1976) so it seems that most people struggle on alone. This estimate is probably a little on the low side; admitting to sexual difficulty is not quite as easy as admitting to being a poor cook - even when answering a survey.

The Main Cause of Sexual Dysfunction

The main problem regarding sexual intercourse seems to be that it is neither natural nor easy. The basic sexual responses, such as penile erection and vaginal lubrication, are basically reflective in character, being integrated at the lowest level of the central nervous system, the spinal cord. However, these reponses are mediated by the brain and, therefore, are susceptible to modification through experience:

... the brain watches over the activity of the body and spinal cord like a hawk, and it can modify the patterns of nervous activity throughout the body ... the brain can interfere with sexual patterns that would normally be released by erotic stimuli. (Luria & Rose 1979)

Therefore, we must consider the brain to be the major sexual organ and realise that it is lack of "know how" and worry about sexual performance or bodily imperfections which are the main causes of sexual dysfunction. General ignorance about bodily functioning and the actual mechanisms of sexual intercourse is a major cause because successful sexual intercourse is learned behaviour and it is extremely difficult to learn something which human beings, unlike any other animals, insist on doing in private. Despite the protests of Mary Whitehouse-type campaigners, the media is not awash with explicit, technically accurate sex scenes. What is usually portrayed on film and television is a man and a woman, discreetly covered with a sheet from the waist down or carefully shot to show only the man's behind, who are writhing about and grimacing and groaning. In terms of techniques, this teaches people little although it has, no doubt, quite profound effects on expectations and attitudes, especially as the couple are usually young, beautiful and athletic.

Research into the sexual behaviour and knowledge of young people shows that our so-called permissive society has done little to teach us about the mechanics of sexual intercourse and bodily function. Schofield (1976) found that many teenage girls in his study did not understand textbook illustrations in basic human biology books. They could not identify with the two dimensional drawings, usually coloured purple for some obscure reason, and they complained, for example, that drawings of fallopian tubes looked like snakes. Similarly, the report "Pregnant at School" (1979) found young people, particularly boys, to be appallingly ignorant about basic sexuality and more recent international studies support this finding. The Goldman Study (1982) revealed significant levels of ignorance in important areas; for example, they found that only thirteen percent of English fifteen year olds could explain what a uterus is, and Johnson and Chopra's study of Australian adolescents (1983) found that twenty percent of their sample chose the wrong alternative in fifteen of thirty-seven simple items about sexual myths; the items included such myths as "a woman must have an orgasm in order to conceive" and "a man's sexual performance is related to the size of his penis".

The problem seems to be that sex education is not taught in any coherent sort of way. Pupils get basic facts in human biology lessons, moral issues are taught in religious and social education lessons, health issues are treated as a separate subject and there is also what is picked up at home, from friends and via the media. A study of a school with an integrated curriculum with a heavy emphasis on social and personal education found that the pupils had not integrated the knowledge gained in separate lessons into any coherent set of concepts (Taylor 1984). The proliferation of sex education books and pamphlets for distribution to young people is not without its problems either; a study of forty widely available books (Hill & Lloyd-Jones 1970) found them to be in general inaccurate and misleading.

Whilst there is no real evidence to show that better information could necessarily have a direct effect on successful sexual functioning in adult life, there is firm evidence that better information from adults, followed by opportunities to discuss the information with friends, leads to young people delaying rather than experimenting early with sexual encounters (Farrell1978; Reid 1982). As a general rule then, social workers dealing with adolescents, even seemingly sexually sophisticated youngsters, should presume a fair degree of ignorance and misinformation. They should also be prepared to discuss these areas with young people, especially in group work, as there is little hope that schools will be able to improve matters in a climate of falling rolls, financial cutbacks and teacher redundancies. As pointed out elsewhere (Blyth & Milner, 1986), social services department can, within intermediate treatment schemes, make more provision for small group teaching than schools currently are able to do.

And, before social workers engage in this area, they had better check their own sexual knowledge; myths abound amongst adults too. Men, particularly, seem to be obsessed with an undue emphasis on penis size. This ranges from the comments of teenager Adrian Mole (Townsend 1982), who was constantly measuring his "thing", to Claire Rayner's regular complaint in her agony column that she is of the belief that baby boys are born into this world clutching rulers in their little hand, judging by the number of letters she receives on the subject. Women, too, seem subject to the same sorts of sexual mythology about perfect shapes and sizes; there are particular worries that childbirth might have "stretched" them irreversibly or that they may be "stitched up" too tightly following an episitomy. And, in the search for a perfect female orgasm, Americans are now trying to identify a G-spot, a supposedly small, yet sensitive, structure within the anterior wall of the vagina which is supersensitive to intravaginal stimulation (Ladas et al 1982). They haven't proved its existence yet, but they have got a lot of people worried about possibly not having one!

Another factor which seems to compound the effects of ignorance and worries about bodily imperfections on sexual functioning is the habit many families have of attaching shame to sexual behaviour. A restrictive upbringing which teaches children to associate fear, guilt and disgust with sexuality is not easily reversed. Kinsey (1948) first observed that orthodox Jews and devout Catholics were the least sexually active and this finding has been confirmed by later studies (Masters & Johnson 1970; Hite 1976). Even more alarming, close-knit religious families rate highly in the incest figures (Herman 1982). However, any parent, religious or not, who teaches a child to be ashamed of sexuality contributes to that child's sexual difficulties in adulthood. The move towards making books available to young children which teach them that their bodies are their own and that they should say who can touch them (for example, Freeman, L. (1982) *It's My Body)* is to be welcomed but should, really, be accompanied by texts which also teach children not to be ashamed of their bodies.

Other Causes of Sexual Dysfunction

Issues regarding long-lasting attitudes and a general climate of ignorance may seem to be of only marginal significance to social workers, other than those dealing with fast developing children, but most of the other major causes of sexual dysfunction lie at the very centre of most social work. These involve us in working with people damaged by effects of trauma, adverse family relationships, illness and handicap, drugs and alcohol, and ageing.

Trauma is well accepted as a contributory factor in adult sexual dysfunction; psychoanalytic theory, in particular, rests mainly on the effects of early childhood trauma on later sexual development. Unfortunately, the studies on which the theory rests are retro-spective, non-representative, male-biased and at no point is trauma defined in terms of seriousness or predictability. In fact, in psycho-analytic theory, the trauma or sexual shock is often held to be unconscious wish fulfilment. This is a great handicap because the level of trauma has been found to be variable. Most people suffer some sort of sexual approach in childhood but it is not always trau-matic (Katz & Mazur 1979), although it is clear that serious sustained and secret sexual assault in childhood certainly damages adult sexual functioning (Forward & Buck 1971, Armstrong 1975). Also, the trauma need not necessarily occur in childhood to be damaging. One of the common traumatic experience to affect sexual functioning is interruption of some sort during early attempts at intercourse; e.g. being discovered in a car or overheard by in-laws seem to be important factors which can inhibit later sexual performance (Jehu 1979).

So, social workers need to take great care when they take histories from clients with problems about sexual functioning and they must not ascribe emphasis to any one single factor without good supporting evidence. Even where the effects of trauma seem obvious, they need to allow for the effects of adverse family relationships generally on adult functioning. Men lacking affectionate parents have been noted to develop madonna/prostitute views towards women, hardly a recipe for a happy, married sex life. Social workers will recognise this attitude most easily in the residential care of delinquent boys who often seem to classify women as either mothers or "slags" and have difficulty in working out how to relate to young female house staff as other than "mothers". Women, too, who have lacked a warm, father figure in their lives, tend to have lowered self esteem generally, which adds to sexual dysfunction later in life (Fisher 1983).

As good self esteem is an important ingredient in successful and satisfying sexual activity, the problems for the ill and the handicapped are fairly obvious although they were not tacitly recognised until SPOD (Sex and Personal Relationships of the Disabled - established in 1978 by the National Fund for Research into Crippling Diseases) highlighted the extent of the problems. All handicapped people have more sexual problems than non-handicapped people. People who have been handicapped from birth miss out on chances to experiment with sex, lowered mobility reduces their opportunities to establish sexual relationships, and sometimes they have undergone frequent and humiliating medical and surgical treatment in childhood which affects how they view their bodies as their own private property. Thornton (1981), for example, complains that as a cerebral palsy child, no one ever asked her if she minded her body being touched. She is lucky to some degree; she knows what is wrong with her. Anderson and Clarke (1982) found that many of the handicapped adolescents in their survey did not know the details of their handicap in anything but a general sense, a factor which made it hard for them to develop any sort of adult sexual identity at all.

And, of course, for all handicapped people, there are individual problems concerned with physical comfort and appropriate posture (media messages, in that if they teach anything about sex, teach people that they need to be athletic to be sexually successful), potency problems and emotional problems. Handicapped people have a lower marriage rate than average yet a higher incidence of marriage breakdown (OPCS, 1985).

Any illness which is debilitating, painful or incapacitating will impair sexual performance but, again, fear and worry seem to figure more highly than physical limitations. Although the energy expenditure during intercourse for long-married couples is only equivalent to that of climbing stairs (Thompson 1983), over sixty percent of post-coronary patients have been found to reduce sexual activity considerably or even give up altogether (Felstein 1973). Sexual dysfunction is also more common in both men and women with diabetes (Trimmer 1978) and, although the dysfunction for male diabetics might be explained away by potency problems, the fact that both sexes are affected gives some indication of how seriously morale and esteem are affected in chronic illness, even where it is not obvious physically. A good overview of the sexual aspects of some typical physical disorders can be found in Stewart (1979).

This behaviour reflects the attitudes of all of us, as a society, and the destructiveness of our obsession with the portrayal of only the young and beautiful as sexually desirable. This causes problems to all of us but is especially disastrous for those who view themselves as seriously disfigured. There is a strong association between poor body image and lowered self esteem and an equally strong association between low self esteem and sexual dysfunction (Leahy 1982). People who feel damaged and unlovable find it very difficult to get over their feelings of being discredited as potential sexual partners (Green-gross 1981). And social workers often do very little to help their clients attain a better body image. How many busy residential social workers routinely breach body privacy in their day-to-day dealings with those who are extremely physically dependent? Many social work students spend time in wheelchairs or undertaking "blind" walks to try to simulate the effects of dependency; better, perhaps, to try washing one another and then see what one's feelings are like!

Another effect of social work with the physically handicapped seems to be an attempt to over-romaticise and sanitise the efforts of handicapped people to establish a sexual relationship. For example, a young woman suffering from spina bifida which confined her to a wheelchair and involved permanent catheterisation declared that she was in love with a young blind man she had met at a day centre. Day centre staff immediately wanted them married off and the occupational therapist quickly came up with a well thought out plan about their housing needs and adaptions. Fortunately, the social worker intervened to slow down the "shotgun" wedding although other staff did not like her insistence on asking how the couple would cope sexually.

The couple quite liked this conversation though and, following discussion, the girl went for psychosexual counselling where she was able to discuss the problems which a catheter might create in "petting". The couple saw their most immediate need as being privacy in which to embark on a sexually active courtship, not what level of cooker would best suit them. Accordingly, the lad's mobility problems were tackled by instruction in the use of a long cane and the first journey he learned was from his house to his girlfriend's. There, once a week, her parents agreed to go out to the pub to give the couple some privacy. It all worked out rather well. The couple eventually decided marriage was not for them, although they have since met new partners, but they enjoyed having a "normal" sexual experimentation period and the girl's parents enjoyed their evening out so much that they became less overprotective. If social workers provided more couples with mobility problems the opportunity to experiment sexually and have loving relationships, then the eventual marriages of many couples might have a better chance of stability than they currently have. Hawton (1985) comments:

> Clinical experience has shown that therapy with people
> with physical disability is often very fruitful, and in many
> instances can be briefer than therapy with people whose
> problems are entirely emotional or interpersonal.

Some factors which affect sexual activity are somewhat outside the scope of social work interventions. The effects of alcohol on sexual performance are well known and, equally, medication can have adverse effects, particularly many of the drugs prescribed for hypertension and cardiac disease and most of the psychoactive drugs (DuQuesne 1984). However, much iatrogenic morbidity could be avoided by careful personal assessment and regular monitoring, plus the use of those drugs least likely to affect sexual response or capability (DuQuesne & Reeves 1982). The role here for social workers is to encourage clients to discuss all aspects of their illnesses with their doctors so that the whole person is treated, not just the illness.

Ageing need not be a factor in sexual dysfunction. Quite simply, older men do take longer to get erections but they can maintain them longer and women continue to be multiple-orgasmic although they have fewer muscular contractions during each cycle (Jehu 1979). Yet frequency of sexual intercourse declines with age. Where people are continuously sexually active throughout life, they have few age-related sexual problems; so the old adage "use it or lose it" seems well substantiated. Sexual dysfunction in older people is often related to specific illnesses and their treatment. Menopausal difficulties can give rise to painful intercourse and men seem psychologically as well as physically stressed by the procedures involved in prostate operations. There can be no direct social work in this area but, as well as individual counselling of post-operative patients, there is much that hospital social workers can do in "setting the tone" of attitudes in surgical wards and in helping patients maintain dignity and self respect during hospital treatment.

This very long list of the factors implicated in sexual dysfunctioning makes it obvious that few of us can anticipate a smooth, sustained, successful sex life. Enjoyable sexual activity is so closely linked to body image and self esteem that it must always be rather fragile and often elusive. Masters and Johnson (1970) absolutely believe that enjoyable sexual behaviour is within the capacity of us all and they think that reliable physiological information and removal of the fear of failure will free many of us from the constraints and worries which affect our sexual functioning. They coined the term "spectatoring" to explain the phenomenon of fear of failure. By "spectatoring" they do not mean putting mirror tiles on the ceiling above the bedhead, but rather a cognitive monitoring and appraisal of one's own sexual performance. This, they found to be the biggest inhibitor of sexual activity:

... fear of inadequacy is the greatest known deterrent to effective sexual functioning, simply because it so completely distracts the fearful individual from his or her natural responsivity by blocking reception of sexual stimuli either created by or reflected from the sexual partner".

They devised sex therapy aimed at overcoming this fear and their early success rate encouraged a spate of interest in the treatment of sexual dysfunction which is now generally referred to as the new sex therapies. After the early enthusiasm, criticism has set in. Many methodological flaws have been discovered in their research method (Zelbergeld & Evans 1980) and many of the early good results from therapy have been found to be short-lived (Kilmann & Mills 1983). Whether this is because the problems are more intractable than many sex therapists anticipated or because a paradox is operating, i.e. if the problem is lack of knowledge then increased knowledge raises awareness and expectations, is not really clear. Perhaps we *are* too obsessed with sex.

But to return to my earlier question about whether sexual dysfunction really is a problem and whether it is one for social workers, I feel that we have to acknowledge the contribution of the new sex therapies to our potential for helping people with unhappy sex lives. At the very least, new sex therapy has de-pathologised sexual dysfunction and helped to demystify it. As most of the techniques can easily be carried out by social workers, I shall briefly outline the recognised dysfunctions and the recommended treatment. I shall also mention some techniques which have stood a longer test of time. These come mainly from the field of gynaecology and obstetrics, and the interest of this specialism in sexual dysfunction underlines for me the serious nature of sexual problems. I don't think we are being too obsessed about "good" sex when it is obvious that many people turn up at infertility clinics with as many psychological problems as physical problems.

The New Sex Therapies

Classification of sexual behaviour often seems to be divided into three sub-classes and more recent descriptions of the various syndromes involved in sexual dysfunction are no exception to this human predilection for tripartite divisions. Indeed, the classification of sexual dysfunction is extremely neat, with three matching divisions for men and women. They are typically regarded as:

> impotence / orgasmic dysfunction,
> premature ejaculation / vaginismus, and
> ejaculatory incompetence / dyspareunia.

Impotence is defined by Masters and Johnson (1970) as either primary, "an inability to achieve and/or maintain an erection quality sufficient to accomplish coital connection", and secondary, "a condition in which at least one instance of successful intromission has been achieved". Secondary impotence is considered to be seven times as common as primary impotence but I should think that the incidence of secondary impotence is probably higher still.

Premature Ejaculation is the most commonly treated male sexual dysfunction (Felstein 1978). Masters and Johnson (1970) define it as a man who "cannot control his ejaculatory process for a sufficient length of time during vaginal containment to satisfy his partner in at least fifty percent of their coital connections", and it is considered to be easily treatable. Trimmer (1978), however, rather spoils the "success" story by suggesting that most males start off their sex lives as premature ejaculators and that most improve naturally with practice. Trimmer argues that it should only be considered to be a sexual dysfunction when it continues later in marriage and when the partner complains; thus the condition may be a result of women becoming more vocal about their need for sexual pleasure, and more consideration generally in male-female relationships.

Ejaculatory Incompetence can arise from a variety of physical causes, such as the removal of the prostate when, occasionally, the ejaculate may flow backwards into the bladder, and more commonly from psychological problems. After repeated ejaculatory failure, secondary impotence may develop. From the number of times that prostate operations are mentioned in the literature, I am struck by the sheer amount of hazard to male sexual esteem and functioning in any operation concerning the penis. Perhaps psychosexual counselling should be routine in all genito-urinary wards?

Orgasmic Dysfunction is the modern term which replaces the perjorative word "frigidity". Frigidity implies total blame on women and should not be used as primary orgasmic dysfunction is exceptionally rare. Situational dysfunction is much more common, that is, women who are capable of orgasm but not necessarily during ordinary intercourse (Kaplan 1978).

Vaginismus is a condition in which the vagina contracts to such an extent that sexual intercourse in impossible. It does not happen during intercourse, so dispelling the myth of couples stuck, locked together in some embarassing place. Vaginismic women invariably shy away from vaginal examinations of any sort and are not users of internal sanitary protection. The condition seems to come to light more at infertility clinics than psychosexual clinics, with two and a half percent of couples who complain of infertility being found not to have even consummated the marriage because of misunderstandings about sex or vaginismus (Fairburn et al 1983)

Dyspareunia simply means pain on intercourse. Trimmer (1978) lists three clinical types - superficial, vaginal and deep dyspareunia. The first is usually considered to be psychological in origin but vaginal dyspareunia can be caused by organic and/or psychological factors; for example, insufficiency of vaginal lubrication may be due to lack of interest or result from hormone changes during the menopause, or an interaction between both factors. Deep dyspareunia usually has an organic base such as endometriosis, a retroverted uterus, traumas resulting from clinical abortion or rape, etc.

The new sex therapies available in specialist clinics are basically behavioural techniques devised to cope with the different types of sexual dysfunction, although Kaplan (1978) adopts a particularly eclectic approach. Most clinics in Britain follow the Masters and Johnson (1970) criteria for therapy whereby only couples in a stable relationship are accepted, either heterosexual or homosexual, and where there is a high level of motivation to resolve the problem. Many American clinics accept single people for therapy but this would be fairly unusual in Britain, the main exception being handicapped people who have difficulty in finding a partner.

The basic procedures of sex therapy involve education, distraction from the central problem, increasing self esteem, and built-in rewards and successes via a small step-by-step treatment sequence. The most famous technique is that devised by Masters and Johnson (1970) to combat the effects of "spectatoring". Many couples with sexual problems tend to avoid any activity which could lead to sexual intimacy because of fear of failure and they have often ceased any form of affectionate contact. To allay these fears of repeated failure, Masters and Johnson devised *sensate focus exercises,* also known as "pleasuring".

Sensate Focus Exercises can be described as follows. First of all, the couple are banned from attempting coital contact during treatment and instructed to follow an increasing programme of sensate focus which involves each partner, in turn, touching and stroking the non-erotic parts of the partner's body. These exercises are to be undertaken in warm, private, comfortable surroundings and are aimed at the couple learning how to give pleasure to each other and, more importantly, learning how to accept pleasure. They report back to the therapist/s, who increase the frequency of the exercises if the couple report that they find them pleasurable and are becoming more relaxed. Usually the couple relax sufficiently to break the intercourse "ban" and resume full sexual relationships quite spontaneously. Sometimes resistance to sensate focus exercises is encountered (Hott 1983) and Stuart and Hammond (1980) recommend that mild resistance, e.g. finding it all rather silly, should be ignored or simply acknowledged. More serious resistance, amounting to the sabotage of the programme by one partner, is usually indicative of a marriage problem. In these instances, sensate focus is inappropriate and marital counselling should be the starting point.

The real beauty of sensate focus is that it is fun. Try it yourself - it really is pleasant to be "in touch" with your elbows. And, of course, it is suitable for everyone. Although it was designed for couples who had ceased affectionate contact because of fear of sexual failure, social work students have used it successfully for couples who have never started to have affectionate contact, despite having successful intercourse. Stroking and cuddling are just as important as intercourse for most couples and, therefore, sensate focus is an important ingredient of much social work method.

Systematic Desensitisation is commonly used in the treatment of premature ejaculation, vaginismus, impotence and orgasmic dysfunction. The therapy for premature ejaculation is extemely effective and was first devised by Semans (1956) and later refined by Masters and Johnson (1970). The female partner is instructed to sit facing her partner who is lying down and masturbate him to the point where he is about to ejaculate. She then gently applies pressure to the penis until the erection subsides. This is repeated with the male partner communicating when he is near ejaculation; then the squeeze-stop programme starts again. By this means, he learns the signs of impending ejaculation and how to control it. The couple then move to full intercourse but with the female partner adopting the superior position and not moving. If ejaculation is coming too quickly, she moves off him and applies the squeeze-stop technique.

The advantages of this form of therapy is that it is relatively unthreatening for the man and improves communication between the couple. The success rates with this technique are high although, as mentioned earlier, Trimmer maintains that men are likely to improve anyway and simple counselling and education may well prove equally effective. When the technique fails, it is often due to sabotage by the female partner. Then marital counselling would be appropriate or separate sex therapy for the wife as it is not unusual for both partners to suffer from some form of sexual dysfunction. Masters and Johnson (1970) estimate a probability of forty-three percent; this is not unlikely as people with fearful attitudes about sex and little pre-marital experiment experiences are likely to find each other "safe" partners.

Vaginismus is another condition which responds well to a programme of systematic desensitisation. The basis of the therapy is to start with a tiny object, e.g. the little finger or smallest size vibrator, until the woman is confident enough to accept full intercourse. The key to successful treatment seems to be the initial vaginal examination. Trimmer (1978) suggests that this must be prefaced by a full discussion of fears and fantasies with a full anatomical explanation being given. The use of effective charts is vital here and the doctor/patient relationship must be good. Having coped with a very gentle vagination examination, the systematic desensitisation programme usually proceeds smoothly. However, whilst the treatment for vaginismus is highly effective in enabling intercourse to take place, the woman rarely succeeds in both intercourse and orgasm (Kilmann & Mills 1983). Despite the limitations of this therapy, it remains useful in the treatment of vaginismic women who wish to have babies.

Kaplan (1978) uses systematic desensitisation in the treatment of impotence and inorgasmia. She works on the basis that most people find something sexually exciting and she uses this as her starting point, however bizarre it may seem. She is prepared to see one partner initially, exploring fantasies and masturbatory habits as a prelude to bridging the gap between autoerotic simulation and actual coital contact. She seems to be remarkably successful although I was pleased that her client who fantasised about being Superman did not actually need the costume she was prepared to provide. I envisaged many secondary problems setting in if the poor man had ever attempted intercourse wearing shorts over tights!

Education, present as information-giving in the methods described above, is often a sufficient therapy on its own. Stuart and Hammond (1980) recommend a programme of positive relabelling, permission-giving, communication training, and counselling about fears and guilt feelings. A frank discussion in a warm atmosphere may overcome many inhibitions, especially the assurance that "normal" covers a very wide range. The increased knowledge of human sexual responses from the large American surveys has given us a much better idea about what is "average" but, unfortunately, no one is actually average and much misery has been caused by publicity given to these surveys, especially the stress on sexual athleticism. This emphasis needs to be put in perspective. For example, most marriages are happier before children are born and after they have left home; therefore there are natural troughs in marriage where sexual functioning will be affected by tiredness and lack of privacy. Simple advice about privacy, warmth and comfort should always be tried first; the couple may only need some help with child care, a new mattress or oil on a squeaky door. For people with physical difficulties, education about different coital positions can be helpful as "side by side" intercourse is much less physically stressful than the more usual "missionary" position and is often more pleasurable for women. As this can be hard to explain clearly, a list of useful booklets and associations is offered in Appendix 4.1 at the end of this chapter.

Relaxation Exercises are recommended by Jehu (1979) where a person is simply very tense (see Appendix 4.2). In instances where a woman is worried about lack of vaginal muscle tone following pregnancy, the Kegel exercises (1952) are useful. These can usually be found on physiotherapists' post-hysterectomy and postnatal exercise sheets but are not always explained very clearly. Basically, these involve the clenching of the muscles of the peritoneal floor and, as this cannot be demonstrated, it is easiest described as the deliberate contraction of those muscles which prevent a full bladder being emptied.

Hormone Replacement Therapy is extremely effective in the treatment of dyspareunia although there are dangerous side-effects for the obese, heavy smokers, diabetics and those with a history of heart disease. Itching, dryness, stiffening joints and hot flushes during the menopause are all likely to make sexual intercourse undesirable. However, untreated, a couple who resist from intercourse during the menopause may find later that the husband has developed secondary impotence. Drug treatment for men with a lowered libido is quite useless as there is no known effective aphrodisiac. However, Cooper (1978) suggests that drugs can be useful anxiety reducing agents when combined with a practical training programme. The best candidate for this sort of therapy, he suggests, is an elderly or middle-aged man who really believes that he is deficient in testosterone. Cooper reports that a drug such as Potisan, which is a mixture of testosterone, pemoline, strychnine, and yohimbine, has had some good effects in the short-term, probably because it comes in gold coloured capsules, thus heightening the placebo effect..

Kushtay, a mixture of oxidised heavy metals such as lead, mercury, silver, gold, arsenic and zinc, is an aphrodisiac commonly prescribed by Hakims for Asian patients but it is a dangerous substance. However, Rack (1982) suggests that Hakims are more acceptable than white therapists to Asians with psychosexual problems and more effective, especially as they spend a lot of time listening and are very ready to offer advice.

As mentioned earlier, sex therapists tend to choose their clients carefully and those who are likely to benefit from these therapies in the short-term are people who have only had the problem for a short time, those aged between twenty and thirty, who are emotionally well-adjusted, with a good partner relationship of love, liking, respect and trust, and a history of previous positive sexual experiences (Kilmann & Mills 1983). Oh! that social workers could get such easy clients.

Summary

I am often asked by students in what instances they should try to tackle problems themselves and when they should refer to experts. The simple answer is when the experts can offer something the social worker can't and, in the field of new sex therapy, this is not often. Kilmann and Mills (1983) say:

> ... yet much of sex therapy is educated guesswork.
> Accordingly the therapist is not always able to determine
> exactly the alignment that is just right to keep the client
> on track".

And they stress the need for the therapist to include clients fully in any treatment plan. If this sounds vaguely like task centred social work, then so it is. So why should not social workers undertake it in a thorough, systematic manner? Whilst much of the new sex therapy involves a medical examination and the reassurances this can bring, placing this outside the province of social workers, many people are reluctant to bring their sexual problems to busy surgeries or clinics whilst they are willing to reveal them to social workers who may be working on marital problems or the rehabilitiation of handicapped people.

Annon (1974) suggests a conceptual scheme for sex therapy on four levels - permission giving, limited information, specific suggestion, and intensive therapy (PLISSIT). Whilst the fourth level of intervention is likely to remain the province of the expert, social workers should be able to offer help to clients on the first three levels. They can offer the simple interventions, such as education and reassurance when dealing with adolescents of poor self esteem, marital problems, the elderly and the handicapped. Social work efforts with post-surgery patients are an obvious example also, but so too is residential social work which often ignores the sexual needs of the elderly, the physically handicapped and the mentally handicapped.

Residential care, with its lack of privacy, lack of accommodation, lack of opportunities for relationships in the outside world, tends to compound difficulties for both staff and residents rather than lessen them (Davies 1983). Sex is a common human need, just as is food and shelter, and if social workers do not feel that they can offer help in this area, they can at least refer clients to psychosexual clinics which can be found in most Family Planning Services or they can seek assistance:

> *An important advantage of current therapeutic*
> *approaches to sexual problems is that, by and large,*
> *they do not require an exhaustive training in any*
> *particular specialist field ... it is recommended that*
> *novices to the field should try to use it in conjunction*
> *with supervision from an experienced therapist.*
> (Hawton 1985)

References

Anderson, E. M. & Clarke, L. (1982). *The Disabled Adolescent.* Methuen.

Annon, J. S. (1974). *The Behavioural Treatment of Sexual Problems.* Mercantile Publishing Co.

Armstrong, L. (1978). *Kiss Daddy Goodbye.* Pocket Books.

Bernstein, D. A. & Borkovec, T. D. (1973). *Progressive Relaxation Training.* Research Press.

Blyth, E. & Milner, J. (1986). 'What we can learn from I.T.' *Social Services Insight,* 1(12), p21

Coombs, J. (1982). 'A Seminar Training Method in Psychosexual Medicine'. *Journal of Psychosomatic Obstetrics and Gynaecology.* Vol 1, No 1, p32-34.

Cooper, A. (1978). 'Drugs in the Treatment of Sexual Inadequacy'. *British Journal of Sexual Medicine ,* 35, 5 April.

Davies, L. (1983). *Sex and the Social Worker.* Heinemann.

DuQuesne, J. T. & Reeves, J. J. (1982). *Handbook of Psychoactive Medicine.* Quartet.

DuQuesne, T. (1984). 'Drugs and Sexual Dysfunction'. *British Journal of Sexual Medicine,* Aug/Sept, pp141-142.

Fairburn, C., Dickenson, M. G. & Greenwood, J. (1983). *Sexual Problems and their Management.* Churchill Livingstone.

Farrell, C. (1978). *My Mother Said . . .* Routledge & Kegan Paul.

Felstein, I. (1973). *Sex in Later Life.* Penguin.

Felstein, I. (1978). *'The Needless Misery of Premature Ejaculation'. Pulse,* May 20.

Fisher, S. (1973). *The Female Orgasm: psychology, physiology, fantasy.* Allen Lane.

Forward, S. & Buck, C. (1978). *Betrayal of Innocence.* Penguin.

Frank, E., Anderson, C. & Kupfer, D. J. (1976). 'Profiles of Couples Seeking Sex Therapy and Marital Therapy'. *American Journal of Psychiatry,* 133, pp559-62.

Freeman, L. (1982). *It's My Body.* Parenting Press Inc.

Goldman, R. & J. (1982). *Children's Sexual Thinking.* Routledge & Kegan Paul.

Greengross, W. (1981). 'Sex and Physical Disability'. *British Medical Journal,* 283. 24 Oct.

Hawton, K. (1985). *Sex Therapy: A Practical Guide.* Oxford University Press.

Herman, J. (1982). *Father-Daughter Incest.* Harvard University Press.

Hill, M. & Lloyd-Jones, M. (1970). *Sex Education: the erroneous zone.* National Secular Society, London.

Hite, S. (1976). *The Hite Report.* Macmillan.

Hott, J. R. (1983). 'Resistance to Pleasuring'. *British Journal of Sexual Medicine,* April, pp37-40.

Jehu, D. (1979). *Sexual Dysfunction.* Wiley.

Johnson, S. & Chopra, P. (1983). 'Sex Myths and Adolescents'. *British Journal of Sexual Medicine,* Aug, pp12-16.

Kaplan, H. S. (1978). *The New Sex Therapy,* Penguin.

Katz, S. & Mazur, K. A. (1979). *Understanding the Rape Victim.* Wiley.

Kegel, A. (1952). 'Sexual Functions of the Puboccygeous Muscle'. *Western Journal of Surgery, Obstetrics & Gynaecology,* No 60, p521-4.

Kilmann, P. R. & Mills, K. H. (1983). *All About Sex Therapy.* Plenum Press.

Kinsey, A. C., Pomeroy, W. B., Martin, C. E. & Gebhard, P. H. (1948). *Sexual Behaviour in the Human Male,* W. B. Saunders & Co.

Kinsey, A. C., Pomeroy, W. B., Martin, C. E. & Gebhard, P. H. (1953). *Sexual Behaviour in the Human Female.* W. B. Saunders & Co.

Kolodny, R., Masters, W. H. & Johnson, V. E. (1979). *Textbook of Sexual Medicine.* Little, Brown Co.

Ladas, A. K., Whipple, B. & Perry, J. D. (1982). *The G-Spot and Other Recent Discoveries about Human Sexuality.* Holt, Rinehart & Winston.

Leahy, L. (1982). 'Sex and Disability'. *Social Work Today.* Vol 13, No 28, 23 Mar.

Luria, Z. & Rose, M. D. (1979). *The Psychology of Human Sexuality.* Wiley.

Masters, W. H. & Johnson, V. E. (1966). *The Human Sexual Response.* Little, Brown Co.

Masters, W. H. & Johnson, V. E. (1970). *Human Sexual Inadequacy.* Little, Brown Co.

OPCS (1983). *Marriage 1981.* OPCS Monitor FM2 83/2. September. HMSO.

OPCS (1985). *Social Trends: 15.* HMSO.

Pregnant at School (1979). National Council for One-Parent Families.

Rack,P. (1982). *Race, Culture and Mental Disorder.* Tavistock.

Reid, D. (1982). 'Sex Education'. *Health Education Journal,* Vol 41, No 1.

Schofield, M. (1976). *Promiscuity.* V. Gollancz.

Semans, J. H. (1956). 'Premature Ejaculation: a new approach'. *Southern Medical Journal.* No 49, pp353-357.

Stewart, W. F. R. (1979). *The Sexual Side of Handicap.* Woodhead-Faulkner.

Stuart, F. M. & Hammond, D. C. (1980). 'Sex Therapy' in: *Helping Couples Changes* (ed) Stuart, R. B. Guildford Press.

Taylor, J. (1984). *Sex Education in Schools.* (Thesis written for BSc).

Thompson, D. (1983). 'Sexual Counselling and Cardiac Patients'. *British Journal of Sexual Medicine.* July, pp16-18.

Thornton, V. (1981). 'Growing Up with Cerebral Palsy' in: *Sexuality and Physical Disability* (eds) Bullard, D. G. & Knight, S. E. C. V. Moseby Co.

Townsend, S. (1982). *The Secret Diary of Adrian Mole Aged 13¾* The Chaucer Press.

Trimmer, E. (1978). *Basic Sexual Medicine.* Heinemann.

Zelbergeld, B. & Evans, M. C. (1980). 'The Inadequacy of Masters and Johnson'. *Psychology Today,* 14, pp29-43.

Appendix 4.1

Useful Booklets and Addresses

1. *To the Patient with a Colostomy.* Colostomy Welfare Group,
    38 Eccleston Square, London SW1V 1PB.

2. *Coping with Stroke Illness* and *You and Your Blood Pressure.*
    The Chest, Heart, and Stroke Association, Tavistock Square,
    London WC1H 9JE

3. The Mastectomy Advisory Service, 40 Eglantine Avenue,
    Belfast BT9 6DX

4. SPOD, 25 Mortimer Street, London W1, Tel: 01 637 5400,
    issue free advisory leaflets on:

    > Physical Handicapped People and Sex
    > Physical Handicap and Sexual Intercourse -
    >   Positions for Sex
    > Physical Handicap and Sexual Intercourse -
    >   Methods and Techniques
    > Aids to Sex for the Physically Handicapped
    > Sex for the Severely Disabled
    > Mentally Handicapped People and Sex
    > Your Handicapped Child and Sex
    > Your Disabled Partner and Sex

5. Society of Skin Camouflage, Western Pitmenzies,
    Auchtermuchty, Fife.

6. *So You're Paralysed.* The Spinal Injuries Association,
    126 Albert Street, London NW1 7NF

7. BPAS, Austy Manor, Wooten Wawen, Solihull, West Midlands,
    B95 6BX. 056 42 3225

8. Brook Advisory Centres, 153a East Street, Walworth, London
    SE17 2SD. 01 708 1234

Appendix 4.2

Systematic Tensing and Relaxing Muscle Groups and Learning to Discriminate the Associated Sensations

Tense and relax each muscle in the following sequence for 5-7 seconds, experiencing the feeling, then relax it and experience feeling relaxed for 30-40 seconds. Do this twice for each muscle, then move on. Later, learn to relax merely by recalling the feeling of tension. Then count down to relaxation with the rate of breathing:

i)   dominant hand and forearm

ii)   dominant biceps

iii)   non-dominant hand and forearm

iv)   non-dominant biceps

v)   forehead

vi)   upper cheeks and nose

vii)   lower cheeks and nose

viii) head and throat

ix)   chest, shoulders and upper back

x)   abdominal or stomach region

xi)   dominant thigh

xii)   dominant calf

xiii) dominant foot

xiv)   non-dominant thigh

xv)   non-dominant calf

xvi)   non-dominant foot

from Wolpe in: D. A. Bernstein & T. D. Borkovec (1973)
                 Progressive Relaxation Training
                 Research Press.

Conclusions

In this book, I have tried to look at the social worker's role in sexually variant or dysfuntional behaviour, to examine what we know about the subject and to explore what therapies are effective. The sum total amounts to very little in terms of understanding or changing sexual behaviours. What does become clear, though, is not only the extent to which women and children are abused but also the extreme degree of difficulty which is involved in becoming and staying a successful man in a man's world.

Also what becomes clear is the extent to which our understanding and action in sexual matters has been affected by shifting cultural contexts. Almost all of the studies of sexual behaviour have been done by men about men - largely from Freud to Kinsey. Therapies, too, are influenced by the differing male theorists. Pervin (1984) suggests that psychotherapies flourish in times of social change, when traditional values and institutions are discredited and that particular forms of psychotherapy can give meaning to people within the context of their particular needs and values; for example, psychoanalysis fits the values of individualism, privacy, personal reserve and the management of unacceptable feelings. Similarly, behaviour therapy could be said to have gained popularity because it fits the values of science, pragmatism, action-orientation and a no-nonsense direct attack on problems.

So we may simply have been trying to understand sexual behaviour from a particularly male bias and have treated various aberrations in accordance with particular therapies which have happened to fit our values of the moment. The values and attitudes gaining expression and prominence at the moment are largely feminist ones, particularly as the traditional male medical model is so out of favour. But many feminist interpretations of sexual behaviour are also rather male biased. They all highlight male power and often scapegoat. Herman

(1982) wants to make men more like women by giving them more opportunities to engage in nurturant behaviour; Ward (1984) clearly refuses to forgive them for their behaviour; and crisis centres concentrate on making women as strong as men. What they, none of them, seem to do is to ask themselves why men, who have such power to dominate our understandings and actions, should not exercise this power to make life easier for themselves? Why on earth do men define the successful image of themselves in such a way that so few of them can ever achieve it? They are as hard on themselves as they are on women and as disbelieving - consider, for example, poor Lawrence of Arabia. In *The Seven Pillars of Wisdom,* he describes not only being sexually assaulted by the Bey and his guards but also his later reactions. He does not tell his men what happened and after they moved to a new camp where hospitality was warmly offered, he comments:

> *This was an unexpected generosity, the Wald Ali being not yet of our fellowship. Their consideration (rendered at once, as if we deserved men's homage) momentarily stayed me to carry the burden, whose certainty the passing days confirmed: how in Deraa that night the citadel of my integrity had been irrevocably lost.* (Lawrence 1926)

This is an account which rings true to women but few male historians accept it as an accurate account.

So, blaming men as a species is a pretty unhelpful thing to do. So too is taking over their power - it hasn't done them much good. Also, blaming is likely to make the situation worse. If more men feel threatened, then they will only take it out on weaker men, women and children. Certainly, they will not easily give up their position in the family as it acts as a protection to their mental health. Psychiatric admissions figures show that married women and single men are most vulnerable to depression. And although the family may well have the capacity for the most appalling violence, it also has the capacity for tremendous love, growth and happiness. The problems of being "close up" pose as many questions as "who is in charge?".

For me, the tentative answers lie in some current social work theory and practice. Social workers can continually test out ways of helping people in distress but they need to be freed up from any single mode of therapy and they need to be able to consider the relative positions of *all* family members and the rights and responsibilities of power and powerlessness. Also, they need to be more aware of how the helping organisations usually duplicate the family; they too are largely patriarchal hierarchies and social workers, face-to-face daily with clients, are very junior members of their own family organisations.

Social work theory could, I think, be greatly advanced if a female perspective were more often taken in the first place. By this I don't mean ignoring men but rather highlighting the interesting differences in development. Gilligan (1982) took Kohlberg's (1969) theory of moral development and tested it on boys *and* girls and women. She found that men and women develop socially, emotionally, sexually and morally in quite different ways. Boys learn to separate from their families, particularly mothers, and gain a clear but narrow sense of identity. Girls, she found, developed in a much more connected and intimate manner. She describes three sequences of women's moral development. Firstly, caring for self, interested only in one's own rights, and secondly, caring for others, interested only in one's responsibilities. Development to stage two complements a traditional male sense of identity. Consciousness raising and assertiveness about rights for women will only lead to competitiveness with men.

She describes a third, and more advanced stage of moral development which some women reach. This she describes as a stage of awareness of her responsibility to care for *both* herself and others and she considers that the two sexes can approach mutual understanding when:

> ... *women come to see the violence inherent in equality while men come to see the limitations of a conception of justice blinded to the differences in human life.*
> (Gilligan 1982)

Gilligan emphasises that the state of failing to care for both oneself and others is a state of moral nihilism. She says that studying male development as the norm and always evaluating women's development in male terms of reference has led us to ignore the importance of reciprocity in relationships and the interdependence that people feel towards one another and how we might "manage" this interdependence. I feel that this theory gives most hope for social workers in the field of sexual problems as it offers scope for the development of a charter of human responsibility as well as a charter of human rights. Anna Raeburn (1986) sums up my feelings exactly:

To shake men out of thinking that women are only for worship or whoring would seem to be a good thing but that ignores the fact that we are rendering men impotent if we do not offer them what we seek for ourselves: to be taken as we are found, to be seen as whole people and to be seen as people first and sexual entities second.

References

Herman, J. (1982). *Father-Daughter Incest.* Harvard University Press.

Gilligan, C. (1982). *In a Different Voice.* Harvard University Press.

Kohlberg, L. (1969). 'Stage and Sequence: the cognitive development approach to socialisation' in: Gostin, D. A. (ed) *Handbook of Socialisation Theory and Research.* Rand McNally.

Lawrence, T. E. (1926). *The Seven Pillars of Wisdom Book VI.* Cape.

Pervin, L. A. (1984). *Current Controversies and Issues in Personality.* Wiley, 2nd Edition.

Raeburn, A. (1969). 'Broadsheet - On Men'. *Punch.* March, p36.

Ward, E. (1984). *Father-Daughter Rape.* The Women's Press.

Subject Index